B

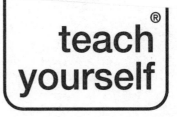

writing a novel

teach®
yourself

writing a novel
nigel watts

The **teach yourself** series does exactly what it says, and it works. For over 60 years, more than 40 million people have learnt over 750 subjects the **teach yourself** way, with impressive results.

be where you want to be
with **teach yourself**

For UK order queries: please contact Bookpoint Ltd, 130 Milton Park, Abingdon, Oxon OX14 4SB. Telephone: (44) 01235 827720. Fax: (44) 01235 400454. Lines are open from 09.00–18.00, Monday to Saturday, with a 24-hour message answering service. You can also order through our website www.madaboutbooks.co.uk.

For USA order queries: please contact McGraw-Hill Customer Services, PO Box 545, Blacklick, OH 43004-0545, USA. Telephone: 1-800-722-4726. Fax: 1-614-755-5645.

For Canada order enquiries: please contact McGraw-Hill Ryerson Ltd, 300 Water St, Whitby, Ontario L1N 9B6, Canada. Telephone: 905 430 5000. Fax: 905 430 5020.

Long renowned as the authoritative source for self-guided learning – with more than 30 million copies sold worldwide – the *Teach Yourself* series includes over 300 titles in the fields of languages, crafts, hobbies, business and education.

British Library Cataloguing in Publication Data
A catalogue record for this title is available from The British Library.

Library of Congress Catalog Card Number: 94-68413

First published in UK 1996 by Hodder Headline Plc., 338 Euston Road, London, NW1 3BH.

First published in UK 1996 by Contemporary Books, A Division of The McGraw-Hill Companies, 1 Prudential Plaza, 130 East Randolph Street, Chicago, Illinois 60601 USA.

This edition published 2003.

The 'Teach Yourself' name and logo are registered trade marks of Hodder & Stoughton Ltd.

Typeset by Transet Limited, Coventry, England. Printed in Great Britain for Hodder & Stoughton Educational, a division of Hodder Headline Ltd, 338 Euston Road, London NW1 3BH by Cox & Wyman Ltd, Reading, Berkshire.

Impression number	7	6	5	4	3	2	1
Year		2007	2006	2005	2004	2003	

contents

	introduction	**ix**
	the apprenticeship of writing	ix
	the myth of the 'writer'	xi
	the importance of being a reader	xii
	three qualities needed for success	xiii
	how to use this book	xvi
01	**beginnings**	**01**
	hardware or software?	02
	a writer in search of an idea	02
	the quality of your story	05
	getting started	06
	practise, practise, practise	12
02	**plot**	**15**
	the three functions of story-telling	16
	holding the reader's attention	16
	what is a plot?	18
	the basic requirements for a plot	21
03	**the eight-point arc**	**27**
	grand, major and minor arcs	32
	analysis of a story	33
	how to use this information	38
04	**sub-plot and symbolism**	**40**
	sub-plot	41
	symbolism	43
05	**character**	**48**
	identification with the character	49
	making characters real	51
	seven tools to convey characters	55
	motivation	57
	representation	58
	know your characters by knowing yourself	60
	roman à clef	61

06   **dialogue**   64
        the three functions of speech   66
        giving the impression of real speech   67
        supporting your dialogue   69
        types of speech   70
        conventions of written speech   73

07   **viewpoint**   74
        types of viewpoint   77
        what tense?   82
        the impact of viewpoint decisions   82
        tone   84

08   **setting the scene**   87
        researching the setting   88
        making scenes real   90
        perception and selection   92
        visualization   93

09   **style**   96
        find your own style   97
        Fowler's preferences   99
        things to beware of   100
        taking chances   103

10   **theme**   106
        subject matter   107
        thread   108
        thesis   109

11   **editing and shaping**   113
        writing and editing   114
        shaping the novel   115
        working chronologically   117
        excision and expansion   118
        pace   118
        handling the passage of time   120
        gaining perspective   123
        novel length and chapter length   124
        finishing your book   124

12   **the personality of the writer**   127
        the sensibility of the artist   128
        the anatomy of the writer   130
        the importance of considerateness   135

13	**support**	**137**
	our physical environment	138
	time	139
	people	140
	writers' circles, courses and books	141
	writer's block	142
	writing as an organic process	145
14	**marketing**	**147**
	going it alone	148
	agents	149
	self-publishing and vanity publishing	150
	presenting your manuscript to a publisher	151
	from presentation to publication	153
	money	154
taking it further		**157**
	recommended reading	157
	writing courses	159
index		**160**

Acknowledgements

'The Hand' from Eating Out, from *I Would Have Saved Them If I Could* by Leonard Michaels (copyright © 1975 by Leonard Michaels) is reprinted by permission of Farrar, Straus & Giroux, Inc.

There are only three rules to writing a successful novel. Unfortunately nobody knows what the three rules are.

Perhaps only another novelist would see the joke, but it's worth telling, because, as with most jokes, there is wisdom tucked inside it. If you strip away the details of a successful novel, you are left with something very simple, and it is easy to believe there *is* a three-step plan to reproducing a successful novel for yourself. Take character 'X', put him in situation 'Y', and make event 'Z' happen to him – lo and behold, instant success, fame, money. If it was that easy, of course, we would all be millionaires. But it isn't that easy – in fact, the closer you look, the less easy it appears. Why? Just because something is simple, it doesn't mean it's not mysterious. A novel *is* simple, just as a flower is simple, but try making one for yourself. We can't – all we can do is to help one grow. We can plant a seed of thought, water it with attention and then we just have to wait. The word 'author' is from the Latin *auctor*, which literally means 'one who makes to grow'. Though we can try to build novels in the way a child builds a sandcastle, at the heart of a successful novel is a mysterious and indefinable 'author-ing', an organic growing of a story. The reason nobody knows the three rules to writing a successful novel is that if there *are* three rules, they are unknowable.

The apprenticeship of writing

Whoever said that writing can't be taught, only learnt, was on to something. What does the expression mean? It means that although writing requires an apprenticeship, it is an apprenticeship whose duration is internal rather than simply a matter of turning up to class. Nobody can teach another person something as complex as writing a novel. The most a teacher can do is to point out the way, make suggestions, indicate the pitfalls and hold a mirror up to the students so they can learn for themselves. And although success is attainable from the very beginning, there is no end to the apprenticeship. A good writer will always be a student of writing.

Rabindranath Tagore, the great Indian poet, was visited on his deathbed by an eminent critic and friend. 'You have much of which to be proud,' the friend said. 'Six thousand poems you have written, each one a masterpiece. You can die content in the knowledge that you have been a flower which has fully opened.'

Rabindranath began to weep, much to the astonishment of the critic. 'Why are you weeping, my friend? Does death frighten you so?'

'I am not afraid of death. I am weeping because I have only just become a poet. Up to now my buds have only been half open. More and more poems are coming to me, each one better than the last. I am weeping at the injustice of being so quickly pruned by God.'

There is no end to the journey towards the perfect poem or the perfect novel. Why? Because no such thing exists. If you find yourself writing and rewriting a sentence, groping towards a perfect expression of what you want to say, do yourself a favour – stop it. Not only can there never be a perfect novel, there cannot even be a perfect sentence. Words are symbols: the best they can do is approximate what we want to say. And just as what we want to say is, hopefully, ever-expanding, so too is our ability to use words which fit. You can learn the craft of writing, but the teacher is yourself. A book such as this one can be invaluable – use it, take heed by all means; however, the lessons will be learnt when you are holding a pen in your hand, and you can become your own instructor.

Art and craft

Another way of expressing this idea is: *You can teach Craft, but Art can only be learnt.* A novel, as any piece of creative writing, comprises two aspects: the craft, that is, the *mechanics* of its construction, and the art, namely the *quality* of its construction. The mechanics of writing can easily be learnt: a page of diagrams can be memorized, a list digested – and you will find both in this book. Quality, however, is more difficult to learn, for it can't be reduced to a formula. Quality is the indefinable mystery of writing, the relationship between words, which is as much the product of the space between words as the words themselves. A mechanical approach to writing a novel will always fall short of what is possible for the form – we can use computer programs to help us with plot ideas and to check our grammar, but no computer can write a good novel, because no computer can understand this mystery.

A good writer isn't just a wordsmith. A good writer is someone who can see quality in the world and can somehow translate that onto the page. Tricky to achieve, but essential if we are to write a novel which touches people.

The myth of the 'writer'

If you are the sort of person to be intimidated by the weight of books that have already been written, or are unsure of your talent or your vocation, take heart. There is no such personage as a 'writer'. If you worry that you don't possess that special ingredient other writers have, particularly the writers you admire – don't. There is only one qualification to be a writer: human beingness.

> I am not a writer except when I write.
>
> *Juan Carlos Onetti*

It took me years before I could call myself a writer, years more before I realized the term means nothing. A writer is a person who writes. A novelist is a person who writes novels. And a good novelist? We're back to the mystery – there is no absolute checklist against which we can measure our writing. Anyone who has received enough feedback – whether from friends or from professional reviewers – knows that everyone has a different idea about what makes a good book, a good writer. If you want a lesson in the futility of measuring up to the notion 'good writer', just try to write something which pleases everybody. It is important to listen to people's opinions, particularly those who have trodden that path before; however, just as the essence of the perfect sentence is ineffable, so too is that quality marked 'excellence'. Why else do some novelists write again and again and again? Not for the money, nor the limelight, nor even because they have a story burning a hole in their mind, but because they are reaching for a distant star, just as Tagore was.

Do I have what it takes?

Leaving aside notions of good and bad, what sort of person writes, in particular a novel? If you wonder whether you have the stamina to complete a novel or the talent to write a good one, there is only one way to find out – write one and see. If you wonder whether the journey is worth the effort, whether you stand any chance of reaching the end, there are some questions you could ask yourself before you start. Do I enjoy reading? Have I turned to pen and paper in times of turmoil? Am I interested in people, and what makes them tick? Do I have a story to tell, or a message I want people to hear? Have I ever been complimented on my writing?

Although there is no such person as a writer, and although people who write are as various as the books that have been written, I imagine most people who have written successful novels would answer 'yes' to most of the above questions.

The importance of being a reader

If you were an avid reader as a child, all well and good (though don't rule yourself out if this is not the case – some of us come to books only later in life). Nevertheless, it is important that you read a certain amount now. This is for two reasons: first, whether you are avant-garde or a genre writer, self-consciously literary or don't know how to define yourself as a writer, you must realize that your work, if read, will be gauged by people who are expert story consumers. Even if your audience hasn't read widely, it is likely it has read a bit. And what about the plays or films your readers have seen? We are the most story-literate society ever – stories are everywhere, and not just in obvious forms. Stories are disguised as news reports and adverts; jokes are nothing but funny stories, gossip nothing but domestic stories. We are experts on our own culture – and although we may not be able to tell a good story, we know one when we hear one. So, if you want to please such discriminating consumers, you need to realize you are part of a cultural tradition. That doesn't mean you have to read all the classics; it *does* mean you can't be completely uninformed. It is no good thinking you are being startlingly original if everyone else thinks it's old hat. It's no good unwittingly conforming to genre and then unwittingly switching in mid-story – readers will accuse you of cheating, just as if you had picked up the ball in a game of soccer.

The second reason you should be a reader is to learn from others. Apprentices work under craftspeople so they can study their technique, and novel writing requires an apprenticeship just as much as furniture making. At first you may find yourself copying other writers, certainly, this was so in my case: my first novel began as a pastiche of many different styles – from Jane Austen to D. H. Lawrence to Kurt Vonnegut. Thankfully, I managed to break free of their influence, but at first it may not have been a bad thing: there is much to learn in terms of syntax and rhythm and authority from all three writers. In the end, however, it is vital that you find your own voice. If not, the story will just be a thinly veiled copy of a better original, whether that be Tom Clancy or Tom Stoppard. Learn from other writers, and by all means (the laws of copyright withstanding) borrow from them, but make your words your own.

A poor poet imitates, a good poet steals.

T S Eliot

Three qualities needed for success

There are three qualities I think an aspiring writer needs in order to have success: luck, talent and hard work. There may not be much you can do about luck (although what some people call good luck in others is often the legitimate fruit of their labours). Talent – the ability to mould quality – you can do more about, although you can only develop something that is already there. It is hard work which is most fully available to us. Writing well is not a doddle. Yes, sometimes the muse descends on us, and all we have to do is hold the pen. Most of the time, however, it involves struggle and discomfort. If novelists wrote only when they were inspired, the shelves of our libraries would be mostly empty.

The importance of stamina

Writing a novel, more so than writing a short story or a poem, requires *stamina*. When I began my first novel, I leapt into it as though I was running a 100-yard dash. A few days passed, a few weeks, and I found myself pausing to catch my breath, looking ahead to see where the finishing line lay. It was nowhere in sight – I had barely finished the first chapter. A novel, I realized, is not a dash, but a marathon. A few weeks passed, a few months, and I realized my metaphor was wrong – a marathon, even at walking pace, can be completed in a day. Perhaps the writing of a novel was closer to an extended pregnancy. A few months passed, turning into a few years and I realized that again, I had got the wrong image. Bar any mishaps, there is something inevitable about pregnancy. If you allow nature to take its course, there is no turning back: a baby will be born. There is no such certainty for a novel. You could work on a novel forever without coming to its end – there is nothing inevitable about completing it.

Courage and encouragement

As well as stamina, you also need something which may not be immediately apparent, particularly at the start – *courage*. Why does writing take courage? Nobody is going to write your novel for you, and it won't write itself. The only way a novel will be written is by you picking up the pen and writing every word – a writer, remember, is someone who writes, not someone who thinks about writing. When the going gets tough, and your story is in a tight corner, or your characters have turned to cardboard, and your enthusiasm to sawdust, there is only one person who can pull you though – yourself. Disciplining yourself to work when you don't want to, climbing back into the saddle when your story throws you, believing in yourself when nobody else does – these things take courage. It is far easier *not* to write a novel than it is to write one. Writers need every little bit of encouragement they can get. So, before you start your project, or if you're in the middle of it, pause for a moment, reach over your shoulder and pat yourself on the back. Even if you're only contemplating writing a novel, congratulate yourself. There are far more people who would like to have written a novel than who want to write, far more people who want to write than actually do so. Encourage yourself regularly in the writing – or better still, find someone who can offer encouragement to you, and you will find that you are a writer.

Climbing the literary mountain

Of the three qualities of luck, talent and hard work, it is the last with which you should make friends. The successful novelist (that is, one who has finished a project which is recognizably a novel) is a stubborn, brave and single-minded individual. Antisocial, perhaps; misunderstood, almost certainly; confused and afraid at times, unsure of their talent, regretful of their mistakes, envious of their peers – a successful novelist may be all of these. But he or she is also a brave pioneer.

It will help make the journey less onerous if you remind yourself occasionally why you want to write. The two essential qualities every novelist needs – motivation and inspiration – are contrary creatures which rebel against coercion. You must coax them, encouraging them, promising them that the journey is worth the effort. Convince yourself that for the person who reaches the top of his or her literary Everest and plants the flag, there is immense satisfaction.

If you have yet to make such a journey, just know that the view from the top of a completed novel is, in my experience, worth the struggle.

No rules

If you learn nothing else from the book, I would like you to learn this: THERE ARE NO RULES. A novel is not a wind-up machine which either works or it doesn't – it is a social convention which is constantly changing. Admittedly, some conventions are so embedded in our culture that we would be unwise to ignore them, just as we would be unwise to drive on the wrong side of the road. But fiction is not real life, and the cost of breaking with convention is often no more than failure to be published. This is part of the pleasure of writing fiction – the freedom from constraint.

If you do want to be published, following the advice in this book will probably help, because the majority of the points I make are a matter of consensus. However, slavishly following a convention is not only misguided, it can be unhelpful: a good novel is a strange thing – you can break every 'rule' in the book and still write a wonderful bestseller. In fact, the best novels are often those which take the biggest chances. It is worth realizing, however, that people who do this successfully are usually experts of the conventions they are breaking. Be well informed, and *then* fly in the face of tradition. Pablo Picasso only became a successful Cubist when he had already mastered classical drawing.

Some of my advice in the following pages is more idiosyncratic, in which case it is even further away from being a rule. But I cannot teach you the craft of writing, because no such craft exists: all I can do is try to teach you *my* craft of writing.

How to use this book

I have structured this book to reflect my own process of writing a novel. Although fiction writing is far too messy to submit to such analysis, my journey goes something like this: I begin with the idea, develop the plot, find out who my characters are, then decide viewpoint, setting and theme. Editing comes way down the line, and the last thing I think about is selling the novel.

Obviously, some writers might perform this process in reverse, so there are two ways to use this book. First, by starting at page one and working your way through it; or second, by using it as a workshop manual, dipping in as you progress with your own novel. The Contents at the front and the Index at the back will help you find what you're looking for.

About the exercises

Each chapter ends with suggested exercises, 'Things to try'. If you choose to do them, a note of caution – don't turn them into a chore. If this happens, stop – it may become counter-productive. But distinguish between a deep-seated distaste for what you're doing and a temporary reluctance based on laziness or fear. If you meet a barrier, and want to stop, try pushing past it. Often on the other side is what you've been looking for.

Things to try

1 Motivation is the key to seeing through the long process of writing a novel. Often we keep our desires as writers secret – even from ourselves. If your desire is buried, so too will be your motivation. Write a letter to yourself, imagining that an understanding and supportive other part of you will read it. Outline the reasons you want to write, being as honest and as ambitious as you want. Keep the letter in a safe place and read it whenever your motivation flags.

2 Choose a favourite novel, and read it again – either in whole, or in part. *Why* is it your favourite novel? Be as specific as you can. What can you learn from it in terms of the novelist's craft?

3 One way of building up your stamina is by doing timed writing exercises. This is a very simple and effective technique. Set yourself a time to write – anything from ten minutes to a couple of hours – then, come what may, write about anything that comes to mind. Write about last night's dream. Write about a recent important event. Write about the room you're in. If you're resistant and blocked, write about that.

This last exercise is not an end in itself, so write quickly and unselfconsciously. It doesn't matter about the quality of what you produce – nobody will see it. Ask your internal critic to step back so you can exercise that most important of writer's muscles – the brain.

You may be out of condition and find you get quickly exhausted. If this is the case, set yourself an achievable target, and then expand the amount of time you spend writing, perhaps by five or ten minutes every day.

It is also useful to vary the times you write. Set yourself the task of writing for ten minutes first thing in the morning, or last thing at night. Write on the bus on the way to work. Write when you're drunk or sleepy or in a bad mood. If you only write in ideal conditions and when you feel like it, you will be like a painter with a restricted palate. You might paint good stories, but they will always lack something.

Two things to remember:

- Write for the length of time you said you would – certainly no less. This is a *timed* exercise.
- Don't read what you've just written. Put it away for a week or two before you read it over. If you don't do this, the exercise may become goal-oriented, and you may fence in your imagination.

'This should be a very useful book for those aspiring writers to whom it is addressed.'

P D JAMES

'Writing a novel is hard, but writing about how to write one is even harder. A book so full of excellent technical advice as this one runs a risk of limiting the imagination; but Nigel Watts avoids that trap, giving the would-be novelist a licence to write with his or her own unique voice.'

D M THOMAS

'There are so many aspects of the text that I applaud, that it's difficult to pick out any single passage . . .

ELIZABETH NORTH

01

beginnings

In this chapter you will learn:
- the pros and cons of writing on a computer or with paper and pen
- how to find an idea for your novel
- how to get started writing and bring your story into focus.

Hardware or software?

You want to write a novel, so where do you start? Let's first of all dismiss the topic of technology. A wordprocessor is helpful: it makes editing easy, likewise printing out copies. Some people find that having, in effect, a neat top copy always in front of their eyes helps them keep their thoughts ordered. A spell checker and word counter are also helpful features.

On a humbler level, paper and pen or pencil have been used, and are still used. Their advantages? They are portable (try using a wordprocessor in the bath), cheap, and have sensory appeal to some writers (yellow legal pads and 2B pencils are a particular favourite). Roald Dahl worked with pencil and paper in his garden shed, a plank of wood for a desk. A novelist friend of mine writes in longhand in bed between midnight and 3 a.m. I am typing this straight on to a wordprocessor, using notes from my trusty red exercise books.

The hardware of writing is largely irrelevant: it is the software (or what in modern computer jargon is being called 'wetware' – the human brain) – which counts. An expensive desk and computer won't help you write (as the best-selling author of the decade, Sue Townsend, found out – she stills finds herself drawn back to the kitchen table). Don't be misled by technology – a writer is someone who writes. Experiment by all means, find a medium that suits you, and then get on with the task of writing your novel.

A writer in search of an idea

So, you have cleared a space on the table, bought your paper or polished the screen of your computer. Now what? There are two ways of looking at this. If you want to be a writer, but have nothing to write about, you'll be like a knight in armour searching for a damsel in distress to rescue. Good luck – there is no guarantee you'll find one. There was a six-month gap between finishing my second novel and starting my third novel during which time I had no ideas at all. In desperation, I scraped around in the department of my brain marked 'good ideas', and eventually came up with a scenario anyone who has read *Crime and Punishment* will recognize. And so I filled a notebook with storylines, flogging this dead horse with diminishing enthusiasm, until one day I forgot to pick up the notebook. About time, too.

It's a frustrating fact of the creative life that motivation alone isn't enough to produce a work of art. We need a spark, a germ, a seed. A novel is not a machine – you can't build one. A novel is more like a bonfire: you can lay as much firewood as you please, but without a spark you'll get no heat. Henry James called this spark a *donné*, a gift, something that you receive.

> We do not choose our subjects. They choose us.
>
> *Gustave Flaubert*

On the other hand, if you are a person who has an urge to bring into existence an idea which has been bothering you, somebody who has a particular story to tell, thank your lucky stars – you have received your *donné*, your subject has chosen you.

Take what you get

Don't resist being chosen. I see it a lot with my students: an idea tugs at their sleeve, but they ignore it because they want to write something more noble, or exciting or intellectual. And generally the results are what you would expect: strained and artificial. But when students recognize the wealth of material they already possess, they can access their greatest asset as writers: their uniqueness. Nobody has lived your story, nobody has had your combination of experiences. Use your life experiences. If you're lucky, you may find you don't have any choice – hopefully your story is demanding to be written.

> You know, you don't always have a choice what you're going to write. You're not like a cow that can give cream with one udder and milk with another.
>
> *Bruce Duffy*

Hoping, waiting and looking

What can be done if you have an urge to write, but have yet to be chosen by your subject? You can hope, and you can wait, and you can look. There is no shortage of material out there, it's just a matter of adjusting your story antennae to 'ultrasensitive'. We are inundated with story stimulus; perhaps the richest source being life itself: real things happening to real people. Form the habit of watching events through a novelist's eye, listening to dialogue through a novelist's ear. My second novel was composed almost entirely of actual events, starting with a chance meeting with a young man in London in a Bayswater post office.

Trawl through your past for story fodder. Particularly if you are writing for children, think back to the events which were important for you at that time of life. The chances are, if they were important for you, they would be relevant to a young reader.

Newspapers and magazines are often a rich source of material. Rather than storing this material away in your memory, or building a stack of newspapers, or files of unsifted clippings, try keeping a scrapbook. Cut out interesting items from newspapers, or photographs of people and scenery that catch your eye. Much of it may never be used, but what you do use can be invaluable. When I was preparing to write my first novel I looked out for faces in magazines which fitted my protagonists. The pictures I settled on – the actors Trevor Howard and Meryl Streep – not only helped me in my characterization, but also provided me with the harmless fantasy of casting these actors in the film version of the book!

A less unwieldy tool in the writer's kit is the notebook – no need for scissors and paste here, just a pen and paper. Jot down snatches of dialogue – both heard and imagined. Write down story ideas and fresh twists in the plot. Sketch maps of the imagined landscape, draw pictures of the house your hero lives in. Some novelists always have a notebook handy, just in case an idea comes when they're away from their desk (which, even for the most assiduous writer, is most of the time). Although non-notebook novelists (such as myself) may admire their more efficient brethren, as long as the ideas are written somewhere (and yes, we *do* use the backs of envelopes), they are safe from the vagaries of the writer's mind: a poor memory. Don't rely on your memory: you may think you can remember it all, but this is the world of dreams we are talking about, and dreams are notoriously difficult to recall.

And dreams *are* useful. If you are a vivid dreamer, get in the habit of keeping a dream diary. I often have story dreams in which I am reading children's books. Although most of the ideas don't survive the transition of daylight mentality (being just *too* way out), those that do have a quirky appeal which is difficult to capture in daylight hours.

I've heard of one writer who uses verbal slips and misreadings to generate ideas. The other day I misheard a passing remark which struck me as having story potential: 'Keep the good worm up', one man said to another. The mind boggles.

A recent discovery of mine is the spell checker on my wordprocessor, which, when it fails to recognize words, will supply substitutes. In this way, my wife's name – Sahera Chohan – was transformed to 'Sacra Choral', giving me a delightful name for a character I have used in a children's novel.

If you have the storyteller spirit, ideas will come along. They may not be quick, and they may not come as expected, but in my experience, they *do* come. Don't lose hope.

> I'm looking for something to write about, waiting for something to happen. I'm waiting patiently like a hunter in a duck blind, waiting for the ducks to fly over.
>
> *Joseph Wambaugh*

Be patient, and like the hunter in the duck blind, keep your noise to a minimum. Perhaps a story is there already and you can't hear it because you're crashing around in your psychic undergrowth.

Generating ideas

A more active way of listening out for stories is by doing the timed writing exercises as described in the Introduction. Ideas for stories can be generated by the act of writing itself. One thought can follow another, and before you know it, you have your *donné*. It is worth realizing that this sort of exercise works best if it isn't goal-oriented. If you're consciously looking for an idea, it may elude you.

The quality of your story

How will you know if your story idea is any good? There is no way of telling, short of writing it, but try asking yourself these questions. How excited am I by it? If it is an idea-led story: do I care enough about the issues it deals with to stay with it for six months, a year, two years? If it is a character-led story: do I have at least one vivid, compelling character?

What about subject matter? Some subjects sell well, some are old hat, but an idea alone won't disqualify – or assure success for – a novel. There are no 'off' subjects, no matter how taboo, or how many times they have been written. Look at the variety of successful novels: though there are trends, they are very general indeed. Originality counts for something, but that doesn't mean the rewriting of an existing story counts for nothing. Don't think of the market at this stage. At the beginning, the person you should be thinking of is yourself. Does the story appeal to you? It is you, after all, who will have to write it. And if a story doesn't excite you, do you really think it will excite someone else?

The first person you should think of pleasing, in writing a book, is yourself.

Patricia Highsmith

Getting started

Research

When you have your spark, then what? The chances are that a certain amount of research will be needed. 'Write about what you know' is an oft-quoted maxim, but what does it mean? Not that you should restrict yourself to autobiography, never straying outside the bounds of your personal experience. If this were so, we would have no Shakespeare, probably no thrillers, and certainly no science fiction. 'Write about what you know' means *do your research*. Some subjects will need less research than others, and for a beginner this may be a significant advantage, but there are no out-of-bound subjects as long as you know what you're talking about. Don't hurry over this stage in your rush to get ahead – the informed reader may find mistakes, and even the casual reader may find the story lacks credibility and depth.

There are two sorts of research needed: external and internal. External research means collating facts about the fictional world you are about to conjure up. If your setting is unfamiliar to you, you need to know about the landscape and weather and culture of the place. If your story features somebody whose background is not your own, you will need to do some homework so that they are convincing. If you know little about the issues covered by your book, do your reading, and speak to people who *do* know.

Internal research is the sort you do without leaving your writing desk. Unless you fully imagine your characters, and how they would react in certain situations, your story might lack depth. Internal research means thinking up their biographies, the sort of people they are; getting to know them. This is my favourite form of research, because it means daydreaming, letting your imagination go. Steep yourself in the reality of the story, try to see the world through the eyes of your characters. If anyone thinks you're asleep, shoo them away and tell them you're working.

How to do research? Enrol your local librarian into your project, and complete a reading list together. Other novels on the same subject are often a good source of detail, as well as the more obvious reference books. Target people who you think have some of the answers, screw your courage to the sticking point (if you're as nervous as I am), and interview them. Try to visit the location of your story to get the feel of the place.

Bringing your story into focus

There are five questions you can ask to help bring your story into focus: what, how, when, who, why? Let's take these in order.

What sort of story?

Do you decide on the type of book you want to write before you begin: short story, novella, full length novel, door-stopper? Comedy, romance, tragedy, farce? Every writer will answer differently – for me, I have a picture of the completed book in my mind before I begin. Somehow questions of form have a habit of answering themselves.

> The form chooses you, not the other way round. An idea comes and is already embodied in a form.
>
> *Michael Frayn*

How do I start?

I am very visually oriented as a writer, and also a lover of cinema, so I like to imagine the scenes unfolding in front of my eyes. I imagine myself in a comfy chair, in a cinema. The lights go down, the credits roll – what do I see? And then what, and then what? When I reach the end of a scene I ask my cinematic sense to tell me what is required next. I rarely fail to get a picture come to mind.

The problems with this are twofold: first, novel and film are different media with different requirements. Some stories transfer well from one to the other; however, there is no guarantee of this. In fact, the surrealist film director Luis Buñuel used to say that only bad novels could be turned into good movies.

The second problem is in recycling cinematic clichés. Anybody who has taught English to schoolchildren will know that when you set them a story to write, it is not unusual for them to recycle what they saw on television the night before.

So, be aware that it is a novel you are writing, not a screenplay, and that just because a picture comes to mind doesn't mean it's the right one. However, if you are having difficulty moving the action forwards, try closing your eyes and visualizing each scene. At this stage, don't worry about comprehensibility – you can edit the day's shoot once you have the rushes in.

When does the story begin?

Sometimes there will be no doubt in your mind. Sometimes – particularly when the story spans years – it may not be obvious. Should you start at the beginning of your character's life, or begin when the main action takes place? There are two main options for handling time.

1 Establish the background (briefly or at length), and then introduce the first important event which precipitates the action, continuing chronologically.
2 Begin at the event and, while progressing chronologically, feed in the 'back story' – the necessary history which places the hero or heroine in context. This is the most striking way to begin a story. Franz Kafka's *Metamorphosis* begins with a bang: 'As Gregor Samsa awoke one morning from uneasy dreams he found himself transformed in his bed into a gigantic insect.'

A third, lesser, option of starting at the end, and then telling the entire story as flashback, is a variation on the two above. Vladimir Nabokov begins *Lolita* this way, the first, short, chapter ending: 'You can always count on a murderer for a fancy prose style.

Ladies and gentlemen of the jury, exhibit number one is what the seraphs, the misinformed, simple, noble-winged seraphs, envied. Look at this tangle of thorns.'

Chapter 2 of the novel then begins: 'I was born in 1910, in Paris.'

If you decide to fill in some of the background, the question is how much to give? Although there are no rules for this, if the event which begins the story (the 'trigger', a term which will be explained in Chapter 3) is not in the first two or three chapters, your readers may become restless. The background of a story is like the backdrop in the opera: interesting perhaps, and able to hold the viewer's attention for a while, but if the overture is too long people will start shuffling in their seats. Most people read stories for the action, not the scenery.

Disrupting the chronology of the story, for instance by starting at the end, or using flashback or time slips is a technique that many writers have used, for example Joseph Conrad in *Nostromo*. This is very tricky, however, and should be used only with good reason. Most novels progress chronologically, and most readers are happy with that.

Who begins the story?

The question of who you choose as your hero or heroine will be looked at in Chapter 8. The person who begins the story need not be your protagonist – in fact, there is dramatic advantage in delaying his or her entrance. J. R. R. Tolkein did this to good effect in *The Lord of the Rings*, building up the character of Aragorn so much that, by the time he was introduced, we could almost hear the drum roll.

Why a novel, why this novel?

The most difficult question, and in some senses the most important, is *why*? Although you may not be able to supply a coherent answer, it is a question worth asking, because tucked within it are other questions of importance, such as: is this the best form for the telling of my tale? Do I have enough material for a novel?

The point of readiness

When is the point you are ready to start the writing? You've amassed a certain amount of research, developed the plot to a degree, have begun to know your characters. At what point do you roll that crisp white paper into the machine and make the first indelible mark? Everyone will be different. Personally, I like to let the energy of my story build until it reaches critical mass, and something has to give. The first word appears, not when I've completed the research, or have every plot event in place – this could take forever. I begin a story when it demands to be written, and this is usually when the characters have begun to live. At this point there is a kind of explosion, albeit quiet, and the story makes a quantum leap between domains. Collation becomes creation, the story is being born. It is both frightening and exciting, for up to this point I have just been preparing to be a writer. Now, I *am* a writer.

If you allow the idea to build to this point of critical mass, you can find that it begins to take on a life of its own. The novel, in some sense, already exists and it's just for you to write it.

> It was as if the novel was already written, floating in the air on a network of electrons. I could hear it talking to itself. I sensed that if I would but sit and listen, it would come through, all ready.
>
> *A. S. Byatt*

How long is the gap between idea and first word? How much time between germination and the appearance of a seedling? In my experience, it can take anywhere between a couple of months to a year or so. This doesn't mean I am doing nothing other than thinking about the project; oftentimes I'm busy with something else. It does mean I'm keeping the idea watered and fed, occasionally checking on its progress. As time passes, so the idea grows and I give it more attention. I don't like to hurry things, but we are all different. There is no formula for this – the thing to remember is that the seed requires a certain respect from the writer. Don't force it, otherwise you may kill it off. And neither water it too little nor too much, otherwise its leaves will wither or its roots will rot. It is a matter of balancing preparation and spontaneity: if you start too soon, it may be premature and you could get lost in the story; too late and you may have no enthusiasm left. Trust your instinct. Remember, a novel isn't a machine, nor is a novelist a mechanic.

Somewhere in here you will realize that any more time spent thinking about the project is procrastination and the only thing left to do is make that first mark on the paper. You may have a fair idea of where you're going, or almost none at all. You will never be perfectly ready, because you can never be fully informed. The only way to find out what happens in the story is to write it.

> Starting a novel is like going to a football match. You may know beforehand what the ingredients are but you still can't tell beforehand what's going to happen. The only way you can resolve the issue is by playing it.
>
> *Thomas Keneally*

So you uncap your pen or plug in your computer. You take a deep breath or two, pour your libations or cross your fingers and say to yourself, 'Okay, I know I don't know what I'm doing, but I've got to start somewhere', and then you fall forwards into the story. And as long as you keep the words coming, they will find their way on to the page, and if you can do this enough – falling, falling, falling – you'll find you've written something which looks like a novel.

Keep it to yourself

In the early life of a novel, I recommend that you keep the idea to yourself. Not to keep it a secret, but because the creative process is private and fragile: premature exposure can kill it off. If anyone asks what you're working on, be vague. It's not that anyone is going to steal your idea (probably), but that your excitement for a project can dissipate if you spread it around too much. One writer likened talking about a novel in progress to watering the garden with a hose and running a bath at the same time: you may find the water pressure drops. Feedback is essential, but now is not the time for it: anything less than a ringing endorsement could fatally wound your passion. Resist the temptation to talk about it – there is plenty of time to harden it up and show it to the world.

Office hours and the muse

Hopefully you will be so passionate about your novel, it will cause you to lose sleep, to forget to eat, and dominate your thoughts day and night. I hope when you sit at your desk words fly from the end of your fingers like sparks. If that is the case for you, ignore this section. For the rest of us, if you want to finish your novel in anything under a decade, you will have to write when you don't feel like it. This means discipline and routine.

Most full-time writers report keeping something approximating office hours, even if it means working the night shift. This is partly true for me, and partly not. Certainly writing is my job, and that involves getting out of bed when I would rather stay in it. However, one of the pleasures of fiction writing is precisely that it is *not* a job. Not that it doesn't require discipline and effort, but that the qualities that stand you in good stead in the office: diligence, trustworthiness, punctuality, efficiency, sociability, co-operation, aren't of much use in the fantastic interior of your novel. There is no point in staring at the page when your brain cells have clocked off and gone home.

Writing is not a business. Writing is an art.

Katherine Anne Porter

A novelist is not a clock-watcher. Sometimes you will write for far longer than you expected, sometimes far shorter. The muse cannot be commanded, promoted or sacked. With training she will be less capricious: if you set yourself a target number of words, or a goal of a certain number of hours, and stick to it, you will find her less unruly. But in the end, she is her own mistress. Sometimes she will dance only if asked nicely and fed coffee and biscuits. Sometimes she will demand attention when you would rather not give it. Try to tame her of course, but likewise respect her whims, for without her, words will turn to sawdust in your mouth. Follow her lead as much as you can. Coleridge regretted all his life that he allowed the man from Porlock to interrupt him in the writing of his famous poem *Kubla Khan*.

How will I know when I've finished?

Don't think about the end of the book. If your manuscript grows beyond 50,000 words it will have the necessary bulk to be called a novel. This process may take you three weeks (as Jack Kerouac took with *On the Road*), it may take twelve years (as did Keri Hulme with *The Bone People*). It may finish with a clap of thunder, it may – God forbid – never finish at all. Now is not the time to worry about any of this. A novelist is an underwater swimmer, sometimes coming up for air, but most of the time swimming in the watery depths of the imagination, just making one stroke after another.

Practise, practise, practise

Writing is not just an art – it is also a craft. Our artistic ability may be given, something we are born with. Our ability as craftspeople, we are certainly not born with: *this* we have to learn. Although some of us learn quicker than others, there is only one way to learn a craft: by practice. And the more you practise, the more you will become a master of the form and discover that words do your bidding like willing servants. The more time you spend at your desk, the less time you will gaze out of the window scratching your head. Set yourself a routine and support yourself to keep to it. Even ten minutes a day is worth doing.

There is a common belief that because most of us are literate and fluent, there is no need to serve an apprenticeship if we want to become a successful wordsmith. We all use language, we've read enough novels, surely it's just a matter of starting at the beginning and carrying on until we reach the sign that says: THE END? That's what I thought until I tried to write my first novel. I soon learnt that a novel, like a piece of furniture, has its own set of requirements; laws of construction that have to be learnt. Just because I had read plenty of novels didn't mean I could write one, any more than I could make a chair because I had sat on enough of them.

Things to try

Some novelists plan assiduously before they begin, some start with a hunch and see where it leads them. Whichever you do, try some of these ideas to help with your story planning.

1 Write the numbers from 1 to 20 on a large sheet of paper, and fill in as many gaps as you can. If you know how the story starts, that is number 1. If you know how it ends, that is 20. You probably won't be able to fill in all twenty, but it will give you a sense of structure and balance.

2 Index cards are useful in structuring the story. Write down as many plot events as you can on individual cards, and then you can change the order if necessary as the story comes into focus. Charlie Chaplin did this – the genius of apparent improvisation and spontaneity was, in fact, a rigorous planner.

3 Never go anywhere without pen and paper. It is at the planning stage that ideas can strike without warning, particularly when you are in the bath, or half asleep, or just about to jump on a bus.

4 List the reasons why you want to tell this story.

5 Some novelists manage to write more than one story at a time – rare birds indeed. If you have more than one idea on the go, or are contemplating several ideas, jot down the outline of each. Which idea does your instinct draw you to? What are the reasons not to begin with this one? Which part of yourself do you want to listen to – heart or head?

6 If you are looking for an idea, trawl though newspapers. Although the news they usually report is grim, there is little doubt that the stories often have dramatic potential. See what you can make of one of the following, all of which are real examples. A six year old girl threw herself in front of a train and killed herself because she wanted to become an angel and look after her sick mother. A man kidnapped the son of a millionaire friend because he was missing his own children.

A man and a woman who met as strangers discussed their separate domestic problems and decided to kill themselves. If one of these sparks your imagination, try exercise 1 in this list of things to try, filling in the missing parts of the tale.

plot

In this chapter you will learn:
- about storytelling as entertainment, escapism and a means to a better understanding of the world
- how to hold the reader's attention and what the requirements for a good plot are.

The three functions of storytelling

What are the functions, for the reader, of storytelling? Although people would express their reasons in a variety of ways, they mostly fall into three groups:

- entertainment
- escape from an onerous or anxious life
- to understand more of the world.

We all know the excitement to be gained from a well-told story, the pleasure of losing ourselves in a book, or of letting slip our worries for a while. And whether or not we are aware of it happening, stories shape our perception of the world. Life is confusing, sometimes threatening; the story can either help us evade this grim fact or help us get to grips with it.

There is a basic human need for fiction, a need which comes on the heels of our primary requirements of food, clothing, shelter and company. There have been storytellers since people had full enough bellies to stop and think for a moment. And whether the tale is told round a camp fire or in the pages of a book, the audience is seeking the fulfilment of these same three needs: entertainment, escape, understanding.

Not all stories will meet these requirements: some are entertaining and nothing else, some leave us more confused then when we started them, some are heavy on understanding and light on everything else. The most enduring stories, those which last over time and are told again and again, fulfil all these requirements: ripping yarns which transport us to another world before bringing us back home with a deepened understanding of this world.

> The story – from *Rumplestiltskin* to *War and Peace* – is one of the basic tools invented by the human mind, for the purpose of gaining understanding. There have been great societies that did not use the wheel, but there have been no societies that did not tell stories.
>
> *Ursula LeGuin*

Holding the reader's attention

Unless the reader's attention is held, the three functions described above will never happen. It matters little how profound your understanding, how interesting your ideas, how exciting your climax, if there is no-one turning the page. A novel, we must realize, only fully exists when it is in the hands of a reader. Until that moment, it is only a potential book.

How to get the reader to turn the page

This is very simple, and like many simple things, very difficult to do. The reader's attention will be held mostly by the author raising intriguing questions and delaying their answers. If you raise a good enough question at the beginning of a 400-page novel, the reader will wade through almost anything to find the answer. (Beware though: if you make the journey too arduous or boring, he or she will probably turn to the back page to find the answer.) Although a single important question may be enough motivation for a novel, significant questions should be raised in every chapter.

But it is no good raising questions if they are immediately answered: part of the reader's pleasure, of course, is in the delay.

Make 'em laugh; make 'em cry; make 'em wait.

Charles Reade

Suspense and mystery

Narrative questions are of two types: suspense and mystery.

suspense ⟶ questions which look forwards into the future for their answer

mystery ⟵ questions which look backwards into the past for their answer

The question that suspense raises is: what happens next? That of mystery is: how did we get into this mess? Mystery is perhaps the more sophisticated of the two, inviting the reader to solve a tricky puzzle. Suspense is more barefaced: this is how life operates – unexpected things happen and we have to take action.

Taken to the extreme, suspense results in the 'thriller' genre – stories which put the hero or heroine repeatedly in danger. The mystery story has developed, at the other end of the scale, into the 'whodunnit', a story which begins with a dead body and works backwards through time until the cause of the death is found. Although these genres focus on their respective questions, both types of question – suspense and mystery – are to be found in almost all fiction. Suspense and mystery can, of course, be used as cheap tricks, but so too, can they be used as the foundation for great fiction. Shakespeare, Dickens, Dostoievsky, Joseph Conrad, Thomas Hardy were all masters of the intriguing question. A storyteller who believes that depth of theme or brilliance of style excuses him or her from raising questions and delaying their answer may be in danger of the cardinal literary crime: boring the readers.

A solved mystery is ultimately reassuring to readers, asserting the triumph of reason over instinct, or order over anarchy.

David Lodge

What is a plot?

Part of the problem we have with plotting is our lack of clarity about exactly what a plot is. We have read enough books and seen enough films to have an instinct for it, but rarely is instinctual plotting successful. A novel is like a long journey: unless we are very sure of the route and where we are going, we will probably get lost. (Part of the fun of such journeys can be getting lost, but it is more often disheartening – in my third novel I had to throw away six months' work because I took a wrong turning.)

The first distinction we need to make is between plot and story. Distinguishing between these two will save many an apprentice writer from wandering too far from the road. We have E. M. Forster to thank for so simply expressing the difference:

Let us define a plot. We have defined a story as a narrative of events arranged in their time-sequence. A plot is also a narrative of events, the emphasis falling on causality. 'The king died and then the queen died' is a story. 'The king died, and then the queen died of grief' is a plot. The time-sequence is preserved, but their sense of causality overshadows it.

Causality is when one event makes another happen. It is these links between events which makes the difference between a collection of anecdotes (that is, a 'story' in Forster's terms) and a novel. Although a story may be interesting, it is rarely as satisfying as a well-constructed plot. Why? Because without causality, there are usually no answers to the questions 'what happens next?' and 'how did we get into this mess?'

Young children have no sense of plot. Listen to their stories: 'This happened and then this happened and then this ...' Love them though we may, there is only so much prattle we can listen to before we tire, for there is no causality in their story, nothing to link these events together. More than the events themselves, it is the links we find compelling: who did what to whom and, most importantly, why.

A plot is like a knitted sweater – only as good as the stitches. Without the links we have a tangle of wool, chaotic and uninteresting. Knitting and purling is a start, but it is not everything. Shape is important too. It is not usually enough to write a series of anecdotes, regardless of their interest, for it is pattern which the eye seeks. Thus 'The king died, and the queen died of grief', apart from raising no immediate questions, still does not qualify as a plot.

So, what *is* a plot?

> A classical plot is a narrative of causality which results in a completed process of significant change, giving the reader emotional satisfaction.

It is worth pulling apart this definition to examine its constituents.

First, we are talking about *classical* plots here. Not that I mean the characters have to speak in Greek, but that the structure is based upon a global tradition of storytelling rather than seeking to forge a form of its own. The vast majority of stories are classical in this sense.

A *process* is an event which occurs in time, and therefore has three aspects: a beginning, a middle and an end. One of the most common reasons for stories failing is the absence of one of these aspects – usually the middle. E. M. Forster's third version of his tale remedies this omission: 'The queen died, no-one knew why, until it was discovered it was through grief at the death of the king.' This has a beginning (the queen dying), a middle (the investigation) and an end (the discovery). And so we have the makings of a murder-mystery with a romantic twist in the tale. Far from brilliant, perhaps, but an improvement on 'The king died and then the queen died.'

This process should be *complete*. A story has no ending other than that of the teller running out of anecdotes. It is a straight line, proceeding into infinity. A plot, however, is a series of loops, very often coming back on itself to complete its journey:

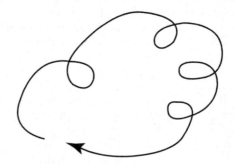

Completion doesn't mean that all the ends should be neatly tied, but that the reader should be able to answer the major questions raised by the author (in this instance: 'why did the queen die?'). The answers should either be explicit (as it is here: 'through grief at the death of the king') or implied. If the reader cannot answer the question, once given all the information, he or she will be confused and dissatisfied. There is an unspoken contract between reader and writer: I will raise questions, the author says, and by the end of the book supply the solution. Failing to supply a solution is a recipe for a disgruntled reader.

The completed process should involve *change* which is *significant*. Stories are a bit like life: events just happen, one after the other. Sometimes there is pattern, but mostly there isn't. (Although I have a writer friend whose life *is* like a plot, one coherent adventure after another which she uses for her next novel – how I envy her!) A plot involves change in the life of the hero or heroine, and change which is something other than random. Of course, the change doesn't have to be in the outer world: many stories leave their characters in the same situation in which they were found. But if there is no external change, it must be inside, for change there must be. The central character should be a different person at the end of the tale – if only sadder and wiser. If the novel charts the journey of characters from point A to point B, B can be anything: happy, sad, up, down. Anything, that is, apart from one thing: A. If the characters are left where they began, the reader will say 'nice scenery, but so what? We didn't go anywhere.'

The result of this journey should be capable of *emotionally satisfying* us. Classic fiction, even of the highest calibre, should be an emotional experience. Not that it needs to be cathartic (literally 'purging the emotions by tragedy'), nor grandly emotive, but it should appeal first to the heart and *then* to the head. If the head is the prime target, perhaps an essay would be the better vehicle. And although we may be unsettled by a novel, weep our way through it or be driven to outrage, the overall emotion we feel when we close its cover should be one of satisfaction. If you quiz a reader about the source of this pleasure they may mention setting, characterization, the author's style; however, if you dig deeper you may find it is simply their enjoyment of answering a question that was raised in the story. This satisfaction is, at heart, what I think almost all readers are looking for. A good answer to a narrative question is as satisfying as scratching an itch.

There is only one story

All classic stories, whether they qualify as plots or not, are *quests*. Somebody wants something and goes on a journey to get it. The thing being sought will be different from story to story – some quests are for survival, some for money, some for relationships, some to return to normal. The characters either succeed, or fail, or get something between the two. Full stop.

The basic requirements for a plot

A *good* story needs a plot, and a good plot needs interesting questions and plausible answers, and four basic requirements.

1 At least two characters

As human beings are your audience, they are your subject. Even though your characters may be disguised as computers (Hal from *2001*), seagulls (*Jonathan Livingstone Seagull*), rabbits (*Watership Down*) or aliens (*E.T.*), they are in effect human, or quasi-human. Just as there is only one story, so there is only one subject matter of fiction: the human condition. A plot, therefore, needs people.

Why two characters? Why not just one against the world? For two reasons: the first is because personal relationships are at the heart of the human condition, even if only by their absence. There is nothing so necessary for psychic health as other people – even Robinson Crusoe needed Man Friday. A world without other people would be barren and featureless. (I have yet to come across a story with only one character. Stories featuring the last man on Earth, or in the case of Paul Sayer's *The Comforts of Madness*, a catatonic hero, are populated by other people in the form of memories.)

The second reason you need at least two characters is because your job as a writer is to make life difficult for your characters, and there is no greater source of difficulty than other people. Hell, as Jean-Paul Sartre wrote, is other people.

2 A protagonist or protagonists

A classic plot needs to have an identifiable protagonist, the focus of attention – the *who* of the story. There are three options available: single, dual and multiple. More will be said of this in Chapter 8.

3 An issue which involves conflict

If a hero attains the goal of his quest immediately there is no story. Therefore, we need obstacles on the way – people, things, events which block his smooth progress. A plot is a completed process of *change*, and important change in the fictional world only comes about though conflict. Things may happen by happy coincidence in your story, but if everything goes the character's way the reader will soon be bored. And if the important change happens easily and with no conflict, the reader will feel cheated. Imagine a story with no locked doors, no nasty surprises, no difficult decisions.

Conflict doesn't have to be on a grand scale – war, for instance, or death and destruction. The difficult decisions don't have to be life-or-death. Conflict can be internal or quiet, as in the novels of Anita Brookner, but even so, it must be there.

One of the things many readers seek from books is to understand life better, particularly its frightening or painful or confusing aspects. The first stories – myths – were told for this reason, and things haven't changed that much. If we want to understand our lives, we have to understand conflict.

4 Some sorts of resolution of that conflict

Resolution requires that all important choices have been made, and there are no significant options left for the protagonist. It is no good finishing a thriller with a loaded gun still in the drawer. Every bullet must be fired, every option exhausted.

Tragedy has traditionally ended in death, which neatly removes the options for at least one character, but beware using it as an easy escape from a tight corner. Death in itself doesn't resolve the plot, except in a very crude way. If the protagonist is left alive and in the midst of remaining conflict, as is often the case in modern literature, there is an important question the author must ask: has the major conflict been completely or substantially resolved? This may not be immediately apparent, particularly if the conflict is internal. You will know the answer to this only if you know what quest your characters are on. It may be a happy ending with the holy grail having been found; it may be a tragedy, the protagonist's hopes dashed; it may fall between the two, sweet-sour or irony.

Whichever of the three options is chosen, it doesn't necessarily mean the end of trouble, but the return to some sort of plateau for the protagonist, even if it is lower than where he began. Unless the major conflict is resolved, the plot isn't complete, and your readers will think that the last page has been ripped out of the book.

It is fine to begin a novel with an accident or coincidence – many stories begin this way. However, if the end relies on chance, your reader will probably feel cheated. The ancient Greeks had a theatrical device we call *deus ex machina*, literally 'god in the machine'. It was a convention used by inferior playwrights who were in such a tangle at the end of the play that only an act of God could sort it out. And thus the audience heard the sound of straining ropes and creaking pulleys and an actor playing a god was lowered onto the stage, where he dispensed summary justice, removed all options from the human players and delivered a platitude or two. Modern equivalents are the cavalry arriving, sundry accidents and diseases, or the heroine waking up to discover it was a dream. I can still remember the shocked disappointment of reading *Alice's Adventures in Wonderland* for the first time:

> 'Wake up, Alice dear!' said her sister. 'Why, what a long sleep you've had!'
> 'Oh, I've had such a curious dream!' said Alice.

Oh no! How could you do this to us, I wanted to cry. You can't paint your character into a corner and then deny the existence of walls and floors.

Two conventions of resolution

There are two conventions of resolution you should know, even if to dismiss them. The first is that of placing the resolution in the hands of the protagonist. There is usually more emotional satisfaction in the protagonist using his or her own skills and resources to resolve the quest than in the all-conquering hero or heroine coming to the rescue. This is particularly important in children's stories, or young adult fiction where the autonomy of the protagonist is all-important – children want literature which gives them a break from their normal disempowered state. The title of Roald Dahl's book says it all: *Danny the Champion of the World*.

The second convention is what in Hollywood films is called the 'obligatory scene.' This is the meeting of protagonist and antagonist, goody and baddy, in the last reel – the showdown at the OK corral. Audiences love this, even demand it, as the famously rewritten ending of *Fatal Attraction* demonstrated: the original ending where the psychopathic character played by Glenn Close killed herself was scotched, in favour of Michael Douglas's character doing the deed.

Sources of antagonism

Just as you need a protagonist, so in order to generate conflict, you need an antagonist. Unless something or somebody opposes the hero's or heroine's will, you will have a story quest which ends before it begins, because there will be nothing between desire and fulfilment.

The source of antagonism can exist on three levels.

1 Inner

The inner protagonist lives within the mind of the hero or heroine and takes the form of an uncomfortable emotion. Psychological turmoil usually looks like guilt, shyness, doubt, self-hatred, fear, anger, a broken heart.

Because the novel (and short story) have the facility of eavesdropping on character's thoughts, it is the narrative form most often used in exploring this internal turmoil.

2 Interpersonal

This is conflict between people, arising from the clash of motivations: character A wants one thing, character B wants another thing which is incompatible. Because conflict between people is usually expressed in dialogue form, this second level of antagonism is most often the focus of stage plays.

3 Environmental

Environmental conflict can either be physical, where a character's physical well-being is threatened (burning buildings, poverty, illness) or social, where a character's social status is under duress (disapproval of society, the consequences of breaking the law). Film comes into its own with third-level conflict – *The Towering Inferno* would have been less dramatic as a novel, and positively dangerous as a stage play!

Complexity and complication

Robert McKee has pointed out that shallowness in a story is often the result of pitching conflict solely on one level: the confessional novel in which nothing ever happens, or the stage play in which people do nothing other than row, or the film whose dramatic focus is one car chase after another. Perhaps the most enduring novels are those which pitch conflict on all three levels: *Madame Bovary*, *Wuthering Heights*, *Doctor Zhivago*, *Catch 22*.

It is not the quantity of action which counts, but the quality. A thin plot is not necessarily made more substantial by adding more action. If you sense this is the case in a story you are writing, pause to consider what levels of antagonism you are employing. If most of your conflict is between people, introducing another character whose motivation is different from your central character's will just complicate matters. Try some lateral thinking: how about an act of violence (third-level antagonism), or a sudden loss of nerve of your protagonist (first-level antagonism)? This might add depth to your plot, making it complex rather than complicated.

Things to try

Being a discriminating reader is important if we are not to start from scratch. We can learn from other writers, both from their successes and their failures.

1 Think of a favourite story (a book, film, or stage play). In what way was it entertaining? Did it offer escape from boredom or anxiety? Was your understanding of the world shaped by the story?

2 What major question was raised near the beginning of this story? What subsidiary questions did the action generate?

3 Was the major question one of suspense, or one of mystery? Were both types of question raised in the story?

4 How much of your pleasure in the story lay in finding the answer to a question? (To remind you of the questions: 'What will happen next?' and 'How did we get into this mess?')

5 Although life rarely has a coherent plot, it often has the makings of one. Many novelists use a true event as a starting point for their writing. If you are not already at work on a novel, try this suggestion.

Take an episode in your life which has dramatic potential. Make any changes to it which could improve the structure – perhaps combining two people into one fictional character, or inventing a resolution. Now write it out as though it is a synopsis for a plot. Ask yourself these questions:

- who is the protagonist/who are the protagonists?
- what is the quest?
- is it more of a mystery or a suspense?
- if you were to write this as a novel, what questions would the events raise? How could you delay their answer?
- what are the sources of antagonism, and on what levels?
- is it completed, that is, are the major questions answered or answerable given the information?
- what coherent change occurred?

the eight-point arc

In this chapter you will learn:
- about stasis, trigger, the quest, surprise, critical choice, climax, reversal and resolution – the eight-point arc
- the structural analysis of a well-known fairy tale.

Every classic plot needs to pass through eight phases, what I call the eight-point arc:

1 Stasis
2 Trigger
3 The quest
4 Surprise
5 Critical choice
6 Climax
7 Reversal
8 Resolution

Stasis

The stasis is the base reality of the tale, the 'once upon a time'. Although the base reality may contain conflict, and indeed an ongoing quest, it is a day much like any other day. Where to start the novel is sometimes a thorny problem. Some novels have an extended stasis (William Styron's novel, *Sophie's Choice*, for instance), while other have only an implied stasis, leaping from the first word into the next stage which is the trigger.

Trigger

The trigger is an event beyond the control of the hero or heroine which turns the day from average to exceptional. The event may be huge or tiny, it may be pleasant or unpleasant, it may not be recognized as significant at the time; however, from this point onwards, the characters really come alive. Before this time, the characters are in suspended animation, their figurative electrocardiographs registering an unwavering line. The trigger is the first blip on an otherwise stable line.

The quest

The effect of the trigger is to generate a quest for the protagonist. In the case of an unpleasant trigger, the quest is often to return to the original stasis; in that of a pleasant trigger the quest is often to maintain or increase the pleasure.

The quest may change throughout the novel. If it does, however, the subsequent quest should incorporate the former, raising the stakes all the time. For instance, a story could begin with the quest for money, evolve into a quest for love, and from there into a quest for survival.

Surprise

A strong quest is a good start for a story, but as outlined earlier, the characters need to encounter obstacles along the way. At the very least, unexpected things must happen.

Sometimes the surprises will be pleasant, helping the central character on his or her way; more important, however, are the unpleasant surprises. The narrative surprises which move the story forwards are, ironically, those which block the smooth advance of the hero's or heroine's quest. Surprise is conflict made concrete, and may be caused by another person or something in the environment; it may also happen suddenly or as the result of an accumulation of events.

For a narrative surprise to work well requires that we balance two things: unexpectedness and plausibility. A poorly constructed surprise is often predictable, visible from ten pages ahead and boring to wait for. Some easily anticipated 'surprises' are valid – I love slapstick, for instance, but even when you see the custard pie coming, the convention demands that the next one will confound your expectations.

It is no good being unexpected, however, if the surprise wouldn't happen within the bounds of credibility set by the author. Implausibility is when the reader's 'willing suspension of disbelief' (as Coleridge called the reader requirement) is stretched beyond the point of comfort. If a surprise is predictable or implausible, the average reader will feel cheated: this is low-grade storytelling.

Balancing the two things can result in the delightful moment in a story when the reader slaps his forehead and says, 'Of course, I should have realized!'

Critical choice

If the unexpected brick wall in a hero's path is insuperable, he comes to a stop and the story is over. If he is to continue on his quest, however, he needs to change course. In order to surmount the obstacle he has to make a difficult decision – what we can call a *critical choice*. 'What am I going to do now?' he asks. 'How am I going to deal with this problem?'

The word 'drama' is Greek, and means 'a thing done'. Not a thing happening by chance, or a thing being done to another, but the action of human beings when faced with obstacles. What sort of actions do our fictional heroes have to make? They have to make choices, that is, they must respond rather than react. What is the difference? It is a question of decisiveness – the hero or heroine decides, whether consciously or not, to take a certain path, even if the choice is to do nothing. The novelist assumes the existence of free will: our characters may be compulsive, driven, inadequate, and deluded, but they must be seen as responsible for their actions, even if their actions are not enough to achieve what they want. Unless the character is accountable in some sense for his or her actions we have accident and coincidence and chaos.

Climax

These critical choices which are forced on the characters come to a head in the form of a *climax*, that is, the decision made manifest. A *surprise* could be a burglar breaking into somebody's house; the *critical choice* of the householder is self-defense, the *climax* is the burglar being hit over the head. Sometimes the critical choice and the climax are back to back, seemingly being one action; at other times there could be a long delay.

A narrative surprise is only important according to the difficult decisions that are forced on the character – the reason why pleasant surprises have little place in the forward momentum of the plot. The subject matter of the novel is the human condition, remember: events are only interesting if they profoundly involve the human protagonists. Intrigue and suspense come from the skilful placing of obstacles in the path of your characters and saying 'Get out of that one!'

The point of obstacles is to put your protagonist in a tight corner so that his or her mettle is tested, so that at the end the protagonist emerges a changed person. Therefore, the protagonist should be forced into making a critical choice (that is, a choice made in the midst of crisis) to continue the quest, a choice which will cause a change of direction.

The surprise, critical choice and climax may be spread over a hundred pages, or appear within the same paragraph. Whichever of these, hopefully the reader is deeply involved in the conflict. Although the focus of the novel may be on the surprise or the critical choice, the climax is a necessary part of delivering the goods. A narrative climax, like a trigger or a surprise, is an event – something occurring in the tangible world of things and bodies. Your climax need not be spectacular, but it needs to be visible. The ancient Greek proscription against portraying physical suffering and death on the stage no longer holds. If your novel is the type to include such things, you should include the crashing cars, the blood, the finger pulling the trigger, not for the sake of sensationalism, but because most modern readers demand it. Omitting a climax, or having it reported, as Sophocles and Aeschylus did, you will be in danger of reneging on an assumed promise: that you will not only supply an answer to the question the story raises, but you will *show* it to us.

The climax is still not the fulfilment of the narrative journey, however. There are still two more steps to climb: the first is what Aristotle called *reversal*.

Reversal

Aristotle defined a reversal as 'a change from one state of affairs to its opposite ... which should develop out of the very structure of the plot, so that they are the inevitable or probable consequence of what has gone before'. A reversal, in other words, is the consequence of previous events – that is, surprises, critical choices and climaxes.

If the climax does not result in a reversal, a question is raised: is there a purpose to the climax other than as spectacle? 'Spectacle' is action for the sake of action, effect for the sake of effect. Elephants in *Aida*, expensive cinematic special effects, the gratuitous sex or violence scene: these are all examples of spectacle, a dramatic resource which Aristotle understandably placed at the bottom of the list. If the answer to the question about purpose is 'No, I just chucked it in there because it looks good', don't be surprised if some readers feel short-changed. Respect your reader's intelligence enough to realize that few of them will be satisfied with spectacle alone. I'm not necessarily talking about literary fiction here: there is nothing high brow about delivering the reader something which coheres into a plot, rather than the 'And then, and then ...' type of story.

If you want to incorporate your narrative climax into the structure, you need to create a reversal from it. This means transforming it from an event which stands alone (and which therefore can be cut without any damage to the plot – which is what may happen when an editor sees it) to one which changes the status of the characters. Some reversals are immediately apparent (the classic tragic reversal is from being alive to being dead, the biggest status change there is), some are not so.

Your story reversals should be *inevitable* and *probable*. Nothing should happen for no reason, changes in status should not fall out of the sky. The story should unfold as life unfolds: relentlessly, implacably, and plausibly.

Inevitability doesn't mean predictability, however. A novel is not a slice of life: it is both more ordered and more unpredictable than that. Predictability has no place in a story: it is what happens before 'once upon a time'. What happens afterwards is drama.

Resolution

Resolution has already been spoken of in Chapter 3. It may be apparent now that what we call the 'resolution' is in fact, a fresh stasis. Our characters return, as it were, to their state of suspended animation, their electrocardiograms finding a new status quo.

Grand, major and minor arcs

The eight-point arc is the classic dramatic unit. A narrative can be divided into constituents, from grand (the story as a whole), through major (the dramatic unit called an 'Act' in theatre, usually dividing the story into three, four or five parts), to minor (scenes). Each of these units, to conform to the classic model, needs to proceed, in order, through each of the eight stages. Progression may be swift or slow, regular or erratic – this doesn't matter; however, if you sense your novel is going astray it will often be because one of the stages has been overlooked. Some omissions are obvious, as in the case of a missing resolution; some are not so obvious, a story, for instance, in which there is no clear reversal. The most commonly overlooked is that of the critical choice.

Grand, major, and minor: these are the three levels the eight-point arc relates to. Thus the arc of a plot could be represented like this:

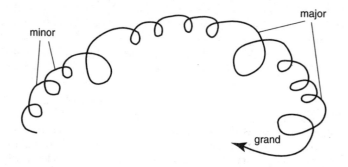

The law of diminishing returns requires that the significance of critical choices, climaxes and reversal increases as the story progresses. If the final critical choice is less challenging than one before it, we may feel let down. If this happens with a climax the result is plain – anticlimax. Pacing is important, combining allegro with andante, as it were, action with passivity. However, anticlimax is rarely successful. The last part of E. M. Forster's *A Passage to India* in which the grand climax (the trial of Aziz) is followed by a quiet (though undoubtedly important) third act, which is in danger of anticlimax.

Analysis of a story

In order to illustrate these ideas, let's strip a well-known fairy story down to its basics and see how it works. Fairy tales are often good models for well-constructed plots: their age and constant retelling have the effect of knocking off any superfluous bits. I have taken the liberty of dividing the story into acts.

Applying the eight-point arc

Children have a very limited attention span, and the stasis of a fairy tale is often a sentence or two: 'Once upon a time there was ...' Children are demanding, if sometimes indiscriminate, readers: they don't want background information, they want action. Thus, the plot proper begins with the trigger 'Milky White gave no milk'. This day is not an average day.

Jack and the Beanstalk

Act I

Once upon a time there was a boy called Jack who lived with his mother. They were very poor. All they owned was a little cottage and a cow called Milky White.

One day Milky White gave no milk. 'There is only one thing to do,' cried Jack's mother. 'You must take the cow to market to sell.'

Off Jack went. On the way he met a strange old man who offered five magic beans for the cow. Jack wasn't sure this was such a good thing, but they *were* magic beans, so he decided to make the swap.

At home his mother was livid. She threw the beans out of the window, boxed Jack's ears and sent him to bed. Jack was distraught.

Act II

In the morning they saw that a huge beanstalk had grown in the night. Without a second thought Jack climbed the beanstalk and found himself in a land high above his own. He walked to an enormous house and met an ogre's wife. She fed the boy and then hid him when the ogre came in for his breakfast. The ogre could smell the boy, but his wife convinced him that it was last night's supper. After breakfast the ogre fell asleep over his favourite pastime, counting his gold coins. Jack stole the bag of coins and escaped without being detected.

Act III

Eventually the gold coins ran out, so Jack climbed back up the beanstalk. The ogre's wife was less welcoming now – the last time she let a boy in, he stole their money. Jack convinced her that he was not the same boy, and she let him in. Again the ogre smelled Jack, and this time nearly found him. After breakfast, the ogre took out his magic hen, who lays golden eggs on command.

Jack waited until the ogre was asleep and then stole the magic hen. The ogre woke, but Jack escaped easily.

Act IV

Jack decided one day to go on another adventure up the beanstalk. Certain this time that the ogre's wife wouldn't let him in, Jack sneaked into the kitchen. This time when the ogre smelled him, the wife joined in the search, but they couldn't find Jack. After breakfast the ogre took out his magic harp which sang beautiful songs when commanded.

Jack waited until the ogre was asleep and then stole the magic harp. The ogre woke up and chased Jack. He nearly caught him, but Jack was too quick, and reached the bottom of the beanstalk before his pursuer. Jack chopped the beanstalk down, and the ogre crashed to his death.

And, of course, they all lived happily ever after.

The trigger is like a starting pistol signalling the beginning of a hurdle race, in other words the quest – which in this case is to sell the cow. There is no change to the quest throughout all four acts: Jack wants one thing only – money (or, at least, valuable possessions).

In order to give impetus to the quest, solid motivation has to be established. If the protagonist (Jack) doesn't have enough reason to endure this obstacle course, he will give up when the hurdles get uncomfortably high. Thus, in this story, it is important that Jack and his mother are poor. (They are well off at the end of Act II; that is, until the gold coins run out.) In this regard, this story goes wrong at the beginning of Act IV: there is no reason for Jack to venture into the dangerous arena of the ogre's kitchen – he has a perpetual source of wealth in the hen. His new motivation – greed or inquisitiveness or a yearning for adventure – is less compelling than his original motivation of poverty, and so as adults we may feel less sympathy to his plight. This story could be improved by making it a three-act tale, less repetitive and more symmetrical.

Back in the story, however, some surprises are in store for Jack.

Narrative surprises in *Jack and the Beanstalk*

The first surprise for Jack is meeting the old man and being offered five magic beans for a cow. If he had met a man who bought the cow for £20, as Jack's mother was expecting, there would have been no conflict and, therefore, no story.

A surprise has two aspects: the set-up and the pay-off. The set-up is the necessary preparation, the laying of clues in the text, so that in retrospect they are seen as causes which may have been overlooked. The set-up for Jack's first surprise, as in all fairy tales, is simple: he has no money and has to sell the cow. The pay-off is the moment of impact, when expectations are confounded. Jack expected to be offered money, and he was offered beans – not just any beans but *magic* beans. In jokes, the pay-off is called the punchline.

The most important surprises of the rest of this tale are divided into two scenes per act: the ogre in the kitchen and the results of Jack stealing from him. These can be broken down as follows:

Act II: the ogre comes into the kitchen and smells Jack

Act III: the ogre searches for Jack and chases him

Act IV: the ogre increases his search for Jack and almost
           catches him

The protagonist should pass greater and greater points of no return, facing greater dangers and having greater pressure put on his resources. The Jack story does well in this regard. If well constructed, the pay-off can be deeply satisfying to the reader. The delight for children here is the escalating danger of Jack: the pay-off – being hunted and chased – is not far removed from many adult thrillers. However, for most adult readers, a good surprise requires more than shock alone; it needs to do two more things.

1 Give insight into characters
Surprise on its own will have limited effect, except for young children. Only if the pay-off has significance will the adult reader find sustenance in it. One level of significance is that of the characters: if we view people differently as a result of an unforeseen action, we have something to chew on. How will they react? What will they do? The answer to these questions should leave the reader having a deeper understanding of the characters in the tale.

2 Change the course of the plot
Another, and greater, level of significance is that of the plot. Some surprises in a novel are minor, and have only limited effect; some are the axis of the tale, changing everything that follows. The change should be irresistible and have a certain inevitability about it, as Aristotle said.

Raising questions and then supplying plausible, yet unexpected, answers: this is the job of the storyteller. And a single ingenious surprise is enough to sustain an entire novel. A few writers, mostly enormously wealthy as a result, have built their careers on the success of their surprises: of them Agatha Christie is perhaps their queen. If you want to hear the sound of cash registers ringing, tickle your readers' sense of intrigue and then scratch then in just the right places.

Critical choices in *Jack and the Beanstalk*

Jack's critical choice in Act I is to sell the cow; his subsequent critical choices are to steal the bag of gold, the hen which lays golden eggs, and finally the magic harp. Fortunately for Jack it seems that he was a greedy little boy with little imagination – no genuine problem deciding what to do. Some more challenging critical choices in well-known stories have been: Romeo stabbing himself on seeing Juliet dead; Juliet taking poison on seeing Romeo dead; Lady Chatterley sleeping with the game-keeper Mellors; Raskolnikov killing the landlady in *Crime and Punishment*. The more challenging the decision, the greater the dramatic potential.

Climaxes in *Jack and the Beanstalk*

The enacting of Jack's decisions are:

- minor: to ask for breakfast
  to lie to the wife
  to sneak into the kitchen
- major: to sell the cow
  to steal the bag of gold, the hen and the harp
- grand: to chop the beanstalk down and kill the ogre

Reversals in *Jack and the Beanstalk*

Jack was rich at the end of Act II (the change was from poor to rich, likewise in Act III), not without reason, but because he saw a bag of gold, decided to steal it, and did so. 'Drama' remember, means 'a thing done' – if the ogre had given Jack the money there would have been no critical choice, and therefore no drama. A reversal shouldn't just happen as an act of God.

Nothing progresses in a story, except through conflict.

Robert McKee

What is the major reversal of Jack at the end of Act I? He starts the story as the trusty son and ends as the punished son – the 'change from one state of affairs to its opposite' is from approved to disapproved. Remember that the plot is a completed process of *change*, most importantly the change in character. If your character has no significant reversal, he or she will probably not be more than two-dimensional.

What is the grand reversal of the story as a whole? From poor to infinitely rich, with implications of power – a popular transformation if ever there was one.

How to use this information

Sometimes this approach to storytelling leaves students cold, and so it should. There is a temptation with such a structuralist approach to think that a novelist is a sort of intellectual engineer: assemble enough parts, follow a blueprint, and there you have it: a mechanism capable of flight – a literature machine. But a novel is not a machine, it is an infinitely complex relationship between author and page, page and reader. Though tempting for a neat mind to design the plot according to the eight-point arc, the control to which we aspire is no more than an illusion. For a novel, unlike a machine, is greater than the sum of its parts. The components of a successful work of art combine to produce something else, something beyond our control. A novel must somehow generate enough electricity between each of its components so that its engine starts to hum, its propellers turn and it taxies down the runway. How this happens is a mystery to me. How we can get normally sensible and sane people, adults as well as children, to take seriously something which is patently a lie, is beyond my comprehension. And when readers *do* take a working novel seriously, they feel emotions, sometimes strong emotions, just as they would in real life. I will never cease to be amazed when a reader talks about a scene in a book of mine as though it really happened.

So, how to use this information? Rather than using it to build a story, I find it most useful as a checklist against which to measure a work in progress. If I sense a story is going wrong, I see if I've unwittingly missed out a stage of the eight-point arc. It may not guarantee you write a brilliant story, but it will help you avoid some of the pitfalls of a brilliant idea gone wrong.

In summary

stasis	once upon a time
trigger	something out of the ordinary happens
quest	causing the protagonist to seek something
surprise	but things don't go as expected
critical choice decision	forcing the protagonist to make a difficult
climax	which has consequences
reversal	the result of which is a change in status
resolution	and they all lived happily ever after (or didn't)

Things to try

1 Starting a story is often just a matter of asking 'What if? If you are not yet working on a novel, try this exercise to get you going. Select one element from each of the following categories (if you want more of a challenge, pick them at random):

character	bricklayer, lawyer, computer hacker, rich layabout, trapeze artist
object	razorblade, pocket watch, photograph, bottle of pills, wallet
setting	remote cottage, library, block of flats, high-tech industrial complex, abandoned warehouse

Put the character (your protagonist) in the situation with the object. Somebody else (the antagonist) is due on the scene. This is the stasis. See if you can imagine a trigger which can generate a compelling quest for the protagonist. What can go wrong? How could it be resolved?

If the idea has sufficient life, explore it further to see if you have the makings of a novel.

2 Analyze a story in progress. Ask yourself these questions:
   * what is the trigger?
   * what is the protagonist's motivation?
   * how does this translate into a quest?
   * is there an escalation of surprises, critical choices and climaxes from minor to grand?

3 Analyze a favourite story according to the eight-point arc.

04

sub-plot and symbolism

In this chapter you will learn:
- about the sub-plot and what its functions are
- about symbolism and imagery
- about the significance and implications of your characters' names, titles and 'jobs'.

Sub-plot

The sub-plot is a subsidiary storyline which runs parallel to the main story, a narrative strand that can be taken away without causing the whole book to unravel. A novel can have several sub-plots, developed to greater and lesser extents – and it *does* have a job to do, other than filling up pages. Although a developed sub-plot is unlikely in a short story, it is important in a full-length novel, adding substance to the tale and pacing its telling.

Substance

The first job of the sub-plot is to add a dimension to the story which the main plot lacks. Because fiction is a tidied-up version of life, it is easy to stray into a simplistic portrayal of events which does justice neither to the complexity of real life nor to the intelligence of your readers. One way of visualizing this is by imagining your main character on stage, performing actions under the glare of a single spotlight: the audience will see things clearly enough, but everything will appear flat, all subtle shading and perspectives ironed out. Sub-plot often involves minor characters who, as it were, circle the main characters with spotlights showing sides of them of which we were unaware. This can have the effect of throwing features into sharp relief, making the characters three-dimensional – in a word, giving them substance.

The sub-plot performs this function in one of two ways: resonance or contradiction.

When the sub-plot resonates with the main plot, it confirms our evaluation of the characters and the meaning we put on their actions – in effect, it says the same thing in a different way. For instance, in *Wuthering Heights*, the sub-plot of Heathcliff's relationship with the resentful brother Hindley echoes everything we know about him: Heathcliff is wild, impulsive and revengeful. The Cathy sub-plot, about her acceptance into polite society and marriage to the doting Edgar, likewise resonates with the main story: they both say the same thing – love is stronger than propriety, passion greater than security. Without the sub-plot, the main story could have survived, but only just – it would have been thin gruel indeed.

Occasionally, instead of highlighting aspects of the main cast, the sub-plot throws light on aspects of the theme. In such cases, the theme of the sub-plot works as an analogy of the main theme, for instance, the Gloucester story in *King Lear*. Here, both men believe the lies told by scheming offspring to the detriment of their unjustly accused loyal child. The theme of the main plot, that of believing flattery at one's peril, is echoed by the sub-plot.

When the sub-plot contradicts the main plot its intended effect is often comic. For instance, in Kingsley Amis's *Lucky Jim*, the sub-plots are strewn with disasters, while the main plot charts the rise and rise of the hero. The hero succeeds, not because of skill or diplomacy – the sub-plot disabuses us of any thoughts of that – but because he is a lucky Jim.

Pace

Sub-plot also has the less complex function of slowing the progress of the main plot. The sub-plot can act as a form of prologue, carrying the reader's interest until the trigger occurs – as in William Styron's *Sophie's Choice*, which in effect has a 100-page stasis about the narrator's past and his struggle to be a writer, before the trigger of meeting Sophie occurs. In the case of an extended stasis, the trigger could be back-to-back with the Act I climax.

Sub-plot is more often found woven within the body of the plot, in which case it can have the function of placing obstacles in the path of the protagonist so that the story doesn't climax too quickly. In *Jack and the Beanstalk*, the sub-plot of the ogre's wife gives additional interest, teasing the reader with questions: will she let Jack in, will she tell her husband where the boy is hiding? Sometimes there is delicious stress in being made to wait.

Multiple plots and two-headed monsters

If a sub-plot is developed beyond a certain point, it takes on a life of its own, and it will have its own eight-point arc, including a need for a resolution. Beware developing the sub-plot too much: you may create a two-headed monster, that is, a story with two distinct plots of equal weight, which can be confusing to the reader. If this happens, you have three options: the first is to reduce the significance of one and increase the significance of the other, establishing an unequivocal top-dog and under-dog story status. The second is to split the book in two and make two novels from it. The third, and most challenging option is to depart from the classic story structure and form a multiple-plotted novel. Julian Barnes' novel, *A History of the World in 10½ Chapters,* is an example of this. If such a novel is to be something more than a collection of anecdotes or stories randomly glued together, however, it must relate *thematically*.

Symbolism

A symbol is anything that stands for anything else. Of course, all language is symbolic – the word 'dog' has never yet bitten anybody – however, the literary forms referred to as symbolism are: metaphor, simile, and allegory. Why do we use symbols? There are three reasons.

1 To demonstrate a concept

Drama is the enactment of ideas as narrative, not the presentation of ideas themselves, which, after all, is the domain of non-fiction writing. Symbolic acts clothe abstract or difficult ideas in form, demonstrating a concept without explaining it. A novel which successfully uses symbolic resonance in this way is Ken Kesey's *One Flew Over the Cuckoo's Nest*: MacMurphy, the troublesome inmate of the mental asylum is punished first by electroconvulsive therapy, and then by lobotomy. These acts, though plausible within the story context, and operating on the everyday level of narrative reality, also have echoes of other things: the first of torture, the second of emasculation. Sometimes a symbol can be extended over the course of a novel, in which case it edges towards allegory. For instance in the Ken Kesey novel, the oppressive State is symbolised by the mental institution which the narrator calls 'the Combine'. Similarly, Joseph Conrad's famously extended symbol, *The Heart of Darkness*, draws parallels between Africa and the dark heart of humankind.

2 To add a further dimension

The second value of symbolism is its ability to add a further dimension to dramatic action by drawing parallels between the particular and the universal. Having a strong symbolic element tells us it is more than one person's story. Seeing beyond the surface reality to what lies underneath, as we do with the Ken Kesey book, we realize it is a tale with social relevance, and therefore something which concerns us all. By showing us the link between the microcosm and the macrocosm, the book steps out of the confines of the page and into our lives.

3 To sneak behind the rational mind

The third value of symbolism is harder to grasp. The more we use words, the more we realize their shortcomings. We may be great experts of language, we may have huge vocabularies, however, life, it seems, is forever evading our attempts to capture it with words. Why? Precisely because words are not real – they are signs, conventions, symbols. The job of the writer is to grope towards the truth of a situation, in the full knowledge that he or she will never successfully pin it down in words. Symbols, because they recognize this fact (love is not at all like a rose, nor the moon like a balloon), can approach things side on, sneaking behind the rational mind in the hope of catching us unawares.

> I am an artist ... and therefore a liar. Distrust everything I say. I am telling the truth. The only truth I can understand or express is, logically defined, a lie. Psychologically defined, a symbol. Aesthetically defined, a metaphor.
>
> *Ursula LeGuin*

But beware: a novelist should make his spade a spade before he makes it a symbol. If it is too obvious or cumbersome, it will undermine the story's credibility, turning it into full-blown allegory, a form with which most modern readers would be uncomfortable. Symbolism works best on a subliminal level. If we notice it, it will have the effect of taking us out of the story, drawing our eye back to the artifice of fiction.

Names

Be aware of the reverberation of meaning, particularly in names and jobs. No names are neutral in fiction – they all carry the weight of their predecessors. A heroine called 'Juliet', or 'Norma Jean' or 'Madonna' will be obviously referential; one called 'Mary' or 'Janet' or 'Anne' less so. Consider names very carefully, and think what resonance they might have (Mary – the Virgin Mary?) Does the resonance suit your intention? Names can be used in several ways:

- clearly allegorical: 'Willie Loman' in *Death of a Salesman*, 'John Self' in *Money* by Martin Amis.
- suggestive: Mr Gradgrind from Dickens's *Hard Times*, Nurse Ratched (a combination of wretched, ratchet and rat shit) and Billy Bibbet (rabbit, baby's bib) from *One Flew Over the Cuckoo's Nest*.

The title

The most important name in the book is the title. Sometimes authors begin with the title and work their way towards it, sometimes the book is written and they are still groping for what to call it. There may be no advantage either way; however, delaying it until the book is finished is a little like calling a child 'Hey you' until it's two years old. A name is not just a facility to help us refer to things: names have layer upon layer of meaning, and they confer dignity. Search out names, both for your book and your characters. Don't force anything, but neither leave it to the last.

> The title of a novel is part of the text – the first part of it, in fact, that we encounter – and therefore has considerable power to attract and condition the reader's attention.

> *David Lodge*

There is no copyright on the title of a book, so you can choose any name you want. It's worth checking, however, with *Books in Print* to see if anyone has got there before you. I think Colin Wilson erred in naming his book *The Outsider*: Albert Camus had so famously made the title his own (though admittedly called *L'Etranger* in its original French) that only confusion in the public's mind could ensue.

Occasionally a publisher will want you to change the title. Be amenable: publishers probably know what they are doing. However, if you really believe in it, stick to your guns. It is only through author intransigence that such wonders as *V* and *By Grand Central Station I sat down and wept* come into existence. Though the reviewers, and sometimes your publishers too, will misquote the title, at least you have named your baby the way you wanted.

Jobs

The first question most people ask on meeting a stranger at a party is their name. The second is their occupation. What we do for a living, they way we spend our day, our social status – these are all important indicators to the type of person we are being introduced to.

Nothing is by chance in fiction; however, jobs of your characters have a high degree of significance. If your heroine is a waitress, you are not just saying she is poorly paid, but that she is also a servant; if she is a judge, she is not only a well-paid professional, but the implication is one of trustworthiness and judiciousness. Of course, you may use this to trick the reader: a judge called Prudence Bold may in fact be a perjuring and corrupt hypocrite. Again, use this cautiously (you couldn't have a judge called Prudence Bold – it is too obvious).

Imagery

There is a point where symbolism merges into imagery, that is, the painting of pictures with words. When this happens we have to leave logic behind and feel our way aesthetically. D. H. Lawrence was a master of powerful imagery – industrial towns, galloping horses, wrestling men. In *Lady Chatterley's Lover*, the high-class mistress falls in love with a gamekeeper, a man not just of a different class but one with dirt under his fingernails. Is this symbolic, or just a wonderful picture? The fact that her husband, Clifford Chatterley, had been crippled (and made impotent) in the Great War, fighting on behalf of the industrial-military complex is significant, but it doesn't matter whether it is a symbol or not. Mellors, the gamekeeper, is his opposite: proletarian, agrarian and potent. There is no doubt what Lawrence is telling us about the bigger picture: the modern age is emasculating men.

The wonderful lie which was published under the title *Lady Chatterley's Lover* is a work of art, and it has a truth beyond documentary; an aesthetic truth which can be expressed only through symbols and metaphors.

Things to try

1 If you are working on a novel, examine the main plot. Ask yourself what attributes of your main cast need to be highlighted by sub-plot. Are you going to do this by resonance or by contradiction?

2 Examine your sub-plot. What function is it fulfilling? How could it be developed in order to contribute more to the telling of the main plot?

3 Are there any unwittingly symbolic elements in your story? If so, are they congruent with what you want to say? If not, what alterations could you make to bring all elements into alignment?

4 Take these one-line synopses (with possible themes in brackets) and invent a sub-plot to complement them (either by resonance or by contradiction):

A father and son successfully cope with the aftermath of a divorce, but then the mother fights for custody (love has responsibilities).

An out-of-work actor impersonates a woman to get work, and becomes a soap-opera star (men are very different from women).

A young man follows his heart rather than adult expectations (freedom is more important than responsibility).

If you want to see what one story medium has made of these ideas, study the Dustin Hoffman films: *Kramer Vs Kramer*, *Tootsie* and *The Graduate*, from which I took the outlines. Because of the rigorous financial and technical constraints of cinema, films often display very precise story structures, and as novelists we can often benefit from studying them.

5 Write down the name of the cast – or intended cast – of your novel. Beside each name, list the resonance the names bring to mind.

6 Do the same with a favourite novel.

7 If you haven't decided the title of a work in progress, brainstorm some options and try them out on people. Ask what the title makes them think of.

character

In this chapter you will learn:
- about how and why we identify with certain characters
- how to establish 'real' characters and then change them (for good or bad) during the course of the story
- about *roman à clef*.

In his *Poetics*, Aristotle declared that the hierarchy of dramatic effects was in descending order as follows: plot, character, dialogue, music and spectacle. (The novelistic equivalent of music is perhaps style; spectacle has already been spoken of.) E. M. Forster disagreed, considering character to be more important that plot. It was Henry James who pointed out that plot and character are one and the same.

> What is character but the determination of incident? What is incident but the illustration of character?
>
> *Henry James*

Authors tend to find their novels fall into one of two camps which they may swap between from book to book: the character-led story and the plot-led story. Characters, if they are strong enough, can evolve into pseudo-autonomous beings who are resilient enough to lead the author through the twists and turns of plot. It can be fun to travel this way, because we never know what is around the next turning. However, if as has been said, plot is the footprints of your characters in the snow, following the lead of your characters can mean a chaotic and slushy mess. It is not enough to have characters move aimlessly though a story; pattern is required, as is some sort of character change by the end of the narrative. Characters who do not learn from their experiences are most often found in the monotony of soap opera, tracing and retracing their steps until killed off by the scriptwriter.

You are less likely to be lost in a plot-led story; however, here the characters can become pegs to fit into the slots of the plot. The imposition of structure on your characters can be at the expense of what seems their realness. Although, it is fanciful to say that characters take over (if they do, you had better book an appointment with your doctor), there is a fluidity and liveliness which can be gained by allowing instinct and intuition to guide your writing hand, Perhaps, as with most things, balance is the key.

Identification with the character

It is what characters *do* that makes them interesting, not just who they are. A fascinating character is made fascinating, not because of who he is, but because of what he does. Looking into this matter further, we see that the interest in the character's actions is not so much in the action alone, but in the *anticipation* of action: *now* what are they going to do? As we explored in Chapter 3, a storyteller is in essence someone who raises interesting questions, and delays their answer. The questions, to remind you, are of two types: forwards looking (suspense) and backwards looking (mystery).

How does the magic of suspense and mystery work? How can you prevent your reader throwing the book aside in frustration, or turning to the back to find the answer? This is the challenge facing all writers: to make your reader wait for the answer, and to make the waiting enjoyable. How to do this? By coaxing the reader into caring enough about made-up people, and then putting these people in sufficiently interesting and complex situations so that the reader's sense of intrigue or compassion is activated.

The heart of this is not magnitude of action alone, nor anticipation, but identification. The reader will care what happens only if he or she cares about who it happens to, and this will happen only if the reader identifies in some way with the fictional character.

Empathy and sympathy

Identification happens through two agencies.

1   Empathy

Empathy is recognizing something of yourself in the character. We can empathize with *any* character in fiction because, as I have said, all characters in fiction are human beings, albeit sometimes in disguise. This will always be the case until the first non-human reader is found – until then fiction will always be for people, and about people.

2   Sympathy

Sympathy is liking what you see, that is, identifying the nice bits of yourself with the nice bits of others.

This means that your protagonist (at least) needs to be someone who is convincingly human and appealing in some way. Characters whose emotional attributes are so alien that the reader's empathy is tried, or characters who are irredeemably bad, may fail to engage because the reader is unwilling or unable to identify with them. Without this power of identification, the reader sees the characters for what they are: words on the page with no more life to them than spots of ink.

What about the anti-heroes, the Hannibal Lectors of the fictional world? Even the anti-hero, the villain we love to hate, should have some redeeming features. These are usually power, charisma, wit, style, intelligence. For example, brilliantly intelligent lover of classical music and art – there is something in us which, against our wills perhaps, admires these qualities even in the form of a psychopathic serial killer. The character cannot be too mad, however, otherwise empathy goes out of the window.

Readers must become involved in the story, and this they do by at some level comparing what is on the page with their own experience and saying 'Yes, that fits.' It is not the detail with which we identify, so much as the underlying humanity of the character. This is how we can weep for E.T.'s homesickness and the death of Bambi's mother – characters with whom we share no detail, but with whom we connect on an emotional level. We care about them because we recognize ourselves in them – that is empathy.

Authenticity

The underlying humanity of our characters must be authentic, whether they are humans or aliens. The reader – old, young, wise, naive – is real. The reader knows what it is to laugh, to cry, to hope; knows the inside of his or her head, and will identify only with what is true on the page. True not in terms of the facts, but in essence – what Nathaniel Hawthorne called 'the truth of the human heart'.

> We all know that Art is not truth. Art is a lie which makes us realize the truth, at least the truth that is given us to understand.
>
> *Pablo Picasso*

Making characters real

How do I make my characters real? How do I create a fictional representation of a person who is vivid, knowable, almost seeming to step off the page? Such characters are those whom readers have no difficulty identifying with, and caring for. They are characters who, for the author, seem almost autonomous, guiding the course of the plot, sometimes in surprising directions.

Real characters will be born only when the author knows them at least as well as his or her friends. This means understanding them both outside and inside. Outside knowledge means knowing their physical attributes and public persona. Inside knowledge means their more private and personal side. These two types of understanding can be called characterization and character.

Characterization

Characterization refers to the visible attributes and history of a person. This is often the starting point of getting to know the cast of your story. What do they look like? What is their biography? What star sign are they? What are their likes and dislikes? It is useful to write a profile of each main character in this way – listing as many attributes as you can. Their past, too: what sort of school did they go to? Do they have brothers and sisters? What sort of upbringing did they have? These are enormously important formative influences in the lives of real people. If you want to create 'real' characters, they need a personality and a history.

Characterization, though important, is often overrated by apprentice writers. If we proceed no further than listing their attributes, we can end up with nothing other than a dutiful list of adjectives and still no real live person. Although characterization is useful in giving the reader a snapshot of a person, the image that is created by surface information – the narrative equivalent of cocktail-party chat – will not linger in the mind for long. In effect, if the author supplies nothing other than this, the reader is being asked to remember a list. And lists are notoriously difficult to remember.

How readers read

It is worthwhile considering for a moment how readers read. It is natural to assume that readers have a blank space between their ears, and it is the writer's job to fill in the space with detail. However, if it were as simple as this, then everybody who read the same book would have the same detail in their head. Clearly this isn't the case – perhaps the most striking evidence of this is seeing a film of a book you have read. Sometimes the characters are just right (Bogart playing Harry in Hemingway's *To Have and Have Not* was spot-on for me), sometimes we can't believe the director's choice of casting: we see the same person in different ways. Who is right? We are both right: the purpose of fiction is not to convey facts, that is the job of non-fiction. The artist has far greater licence.

> Artists are people who are not at all interested in the facts – only in the truth. You get the facts from outside. The truth you get from inside.
>
> *Ursula LeGuin*

The unfolding of the novel takes place in the mind of each reader, beyond the reach of the writer. Because there is an infinite variety of people, there is an infinite number of readings. The most any novelist can do is offer stimulus in the hope that the picture evoked is not too different from that intended. Giving an abundance of information can work against the process of visualization, because the more exact we want the picture to be, the more the reader has to rein in his or her imagination to fit with the facts.

Let me demonstrate. Images are conjured in the mind of readers at the speed of light. If you are deeply involved in a novel and you read: 'a young girl came into the room', you will instantly have a picture, albeit ill-defined, of a young girl. Your picture is unlikely to be the same as the author's. If you read that she has a dog beside her, a particular dog will be conjured up for you. Now if you read she is on crutches, you will probably have to adjust your picture considerably – I don't suppose you visualized that in the first place. The more information you read, the more you will have to adjust the initial picture. Take a moment to visualize the girl so far. Close your eyes for a moment and bring her to mind. Now let me add that she is wearing a blue-and-white, polka-dot dress, has white ankle socks, tiny freckles, and a big smile on her face. Oh, and she's eight years old. Starting with a picture and adjusting it again and again is hard work for the imagination. Sometimes our mind refuses to accept the data and we are blind to the fact that the character is eight years old because, in the first instance, we saw her as five.

So, what to do? We need characterization if the reader's imagination is to be guided in the right direction – we can't dispense with it altogether. I recommend you do two things. First, *be as specific as you can*, early-on in the story. Thus: 'An eight-year-old girl on crutches comes into the room. A spaniel is beside her.' If you want, you can add touches at intervals throughout the story, though resist giving anything that requires an overhaul of the reader's picture.

Second, *restrict your information*. Unless the polka-dot dress is important, try leaving it out. It is the truth of the girl we are interested in, not the facts. We can dress the girl according to our impulse, let the reader have free rein unless it causes a serious misunderstanding. In my novel *Twenty Twenty*, I didn't describe my main characters, at all. Does this mean the reader would have no idea of their appearance? I hope not. Hopefully William and Julia, the two main characters, are vivid and realistic for a reader. Is it a problem if one reader sees Julia as red-head, the other as blonde? No.

Why then research your characters? What is the point of knowing their background as fully as you can? This is for *your* benefit, not the reader's. Doubtless you will use some of the information on the page, but most of it will lie below the surface like an iceberg. Unless you have that mass of knowledge, you won't know how they will react when you put them under pressure. In other words, you won't know their character.

Don't worry if you find you can easily visualize your subsidiary characters while your protagonist remains a blank. In real life, trying to bring a face to mind is often easier the less you know the person, while the hardest face to visualize is one's own. If, as has been said, all characters in fiction are aspects of the writer, it follows that the characters closest to oneself will be the hardest to picture. Don't worry about this: it is not the appearance which counts, but the person; not the characterization, but the character.

Character

Far more important than the surface information is the knowledge of what sort of person your characters are. As in fiction, so in life: we make snap judgements all the time using characterization as indicators. However, it is not uncommon for us to re-evaluate this initial decision, particularly when we get to know the person. So, who is the person really? The first impression, or the person we see in action? This is the difference between characterization and character.

Robert McKee, the screenwriter, defines character simply as: 'the choices we make under pressure'. One way of viewing plot is as a narrative pressure cooker. Big or small, personal or global, conflict is at the heart of fiction. And conflict takes its toll on people. It is when people are put under pressure that they show their true colours.

One of the conventions of the disaster movie is the clash between characterization and character. The story starts with

Mr Success ordering people around, but when the pressure mounts, he cracks and shows himself to be Mr Help-me-I'm-scared. The disillusioned vicar finds God, the rowing husband and wife are reunited, the wimp is a hero. True character is revealed by our critical choices, that is, the decisions we make when put under pressure.

McKee says the job of the writer is to:

1 establish characterization
2 reveal character
3 change character for good or bad.

The novel, remember, is a journey. It is not enough to test the resources of your characters if they remain the same people at the end of the story. If this is the case, it is a journey which takes the reader nowhere. And as I said in Chapter 2, the change in the person (that is, the 'reversal') at the end of the story need not be in the outside world.

Seven tools to convey characters

1 Physical description
2 Narrator's statement
3 Action
4 Association
5 Revelation of the character's thoughts
6 Speech
7 Other's thoughts or comments

The eight-year-old girl hobbled into the room on bamboo crutches. The look on her face was that of someone trying to hide disappointment. The old spaniel beside her looked up with rheumy eyes and she crouched to hug it to her chest. The tiny silver crucifix around her neck swung between them. It's my birthday Jojo, she thought bitterly, and I want to go home.

'I miss mama and papa,' she lisped.

Voices came from the hallway. 'I doubt if children in Vietnam celebrate birthdays,' somebody said. 'Aren't they all Buddhists?'

1 Physical description

'The eight-year-old girl hobbled into the room on bamboo crutches.' Physical description is perhaps the most obvious resource. It is not the *quantity* of detail that has effect, as we have seen, but the *quality*. I chose to tell you about the bamboo crutches rather than the blue-and-white, polka-dot dress, because it is more unusual, perhaps the first detail I would notice if I was an observer.

The main advantage of physical description is its concision – you can say a lot in a little space. The disadvantage is that it is passive. Drama is firstly about action. Anything passive comes second. It is, therefore, useful to feed in your description with the action, rather than giving it all at once. Thus I kept her lisp back for a few sentences. The Victorian convention of devoting several paragraphs to giving characterization has its appeal; however, the modern reader often has limited patience. It is the story that he or she wants, and this means action.

2 Narrator's statement

'The look on her face was that of someone trying to hide disappointment' is the narrator's statement. The character of the girl is building: she is disappointed, and perhaps older than her years in her attempts to hide her feelings.

3 Action

'She crouched to hug it to her chest' is the third resource you have – action. Physical action is vivid in a way that passive description often fails to be. Particularly if the action is the climax of a critical choice (and this *is* a critical choice for the child – she is under significant pressure), it can say more than any amount of explanation.

4 Association

This is more subtle: it relates to the setting and the physical detail of the situation and what it implies about the character. A film star leaving a nightclub in the dazzle of papparazzi flash bulbs is associated with success and fame. Jesus riding into town on an ass has the implication of humility. The clause 'the tiny silver crucifix around her neck' is descriptive – we assume she is a Christian, but also associative, particularly in conjunction with the rheumy-eyed spaniel. The girl is meek, perhaps spiritual in some way.

5 Revelation of the character's thoughts

This has a particular value: people may lie to each other, but they don't lie to themselves – at least, not consciously. 'It's my birthday ... and I want to go home' confirms that she is disappointed, and it reveals the reason for it.

6 Speech

Speech likewise reveals a lot. 'I miss mama and papa' gives us more characterization. Dialogue will be covered in detail in Chapter 6.

7 Others' thoughts or comments

These give a different perspective, particularly useful if there is a discordance between the character's worldview and others' worldview. 'I doubt if children in Vietnam ...' not only tells us where she is from, but also contributes to the reasons why she should feel so lonely: not only is she alone in a foreign country, but nobody understands her.

Motivation

You will only know your characters when you know how they will react under pressure. You will know how they will react under pressure only when you know their motivation. What do they want? To save their own skin? To be liked? To get the girl? Everybody wants something in fiction: conflict arises when the things are mutually incompatible, or are not forthcoming.

There is often dramatic mileage in the clash between public and private motivations. When we are under pressure it is our private, undeclared motivation that is often revealed; if this is shown to be at variance with the declared motivation then you have dramatic interest. A character without a degree of internal conflict is likely to be flat and uninteresting. The critical choices characters make won't really plumb their depths, for they won't have any.

When you know what your character wants, you know, more importantly, what they don't want. This is invaluable to you in your role as obstacle-erector, because it means you can invent appropriate hurdles for them. If your protagonist wants to get rich, you rob her. If she wants security, you make her lose her job. An extreme example of a thing which is is not wanted is a phobia, something George Orwell used to great effect in *Nineteen Eighty-Four*, when he invented room 101 – a room full of rats for his rat-phobic protagonist to suffer in.

Representation

Characters in fiction are a work of art, a representation of a human being. To do justice to the full complexity of a real human being would mean writing an infinitely long book – even longer than Proust's *Remembrance of Things Past*. Unlike real people, fictional characters should be fully coherent (though possibly contradictory) and knowable in a way a real person is not. If you endow a character with more than one dominant trait you may find your story fails in one of its tasks: to make the incomprehensible comprehensible. Readers don't want caricatures, but they do want characters of whom they can make sense.

Presenting your characters as too lifelike has another disadvantage: oddly enough, they seem less real. It is like sending actors on to stage without make-up. Far from appearing natural, they will seem pale and ghostly. People in novels are drawn with stronger lines, coloured with richer pigments than they are in real life. They react more violently, have more convictions and fewer contradictions than most real people. They are not real people at all – they are fictional conventions.

There is a balance to be sought here. Colouring your characters with richer pigments does not mean being heavy handed with make-up. Subtlety counts for a lot: less *can* be more at times. Too much of a good thing can turn your characters into an archetype (a typical example) or a stereotype (an oversimplified example).

Archetypes and stereotypes

Archetypal characters are typical examples of a certain sort of person. Seen most often in myth or allegory, an archetype has a symbolic dimension which can be used to a good effect in fiction. If you want to indicate that your novel has a deeper significance than its surface detail, that the individual character is in fact a sign of society and the world, then an archetype may be useful. An archetypical character seems to stand head and shoulders above (or below) mere mortals, for instance Allie Fox in Paul Theroux's *The Mosquito Coast* who at times exhibits almost superhuman abilities. Archetypes can erode the sense of reality you may be wanting to build in the story, an effect you may not always want to achieve. Because of this, archetypes are most often seen as minor characters.

A stereotype has all of the disadvantages and none of the advantages of an archetype. A stereotype is an oversimplified example of a certain sort of character whose representation is not only shallow, but seems to have a flashing sign advertising it. They are flat characters, with no more depth than a sheet of paper.

Round and flat character

The time was when readers would have been happy with a certain amount of flat characterization, even caricatures, in the stories they read. The modern taste, however, is for roundness in fictional characters, at least for the main cast. Subsidiary characters should be flat to a degree: if they are too interesting the reader's eye will be drawn away from the main action and protagonists.

> It is a convenience for an author when he can strike with his full force at once, and flat characters are very useful to him, since they never need reintroducing, never run away, have not to be watched for development, and provide their own atmosphere – little luminous discs of a pre-arranged size, pushed hither and thither like counters across the void or between stars; most satisfactory.
>
> *E. M. Forster*

Charles Dickens was an author who used such flat characters to good effect. By all means try out stereotyped characters for ironic effect, but beware: had Dickens's main characters been stereotypes, he would be just another unread Victorian novelist, for not only would the cast be flat, but so too would the novel. You can get away with flat characters if they inhabit the world of the sub-plot; a stereotypical hero would be a problem. Characters provoke interest only if they 'live' for the reader; they 'live' through the process of identification. It is no more possible to identify with a stereotype than with a mannequin.

If you create flat characters, you must realize they are flat. More often than not, apprentice writers unwittingly create stereotypes, either wholly or in part. The credibility of a round character can be damaged if he is prone to stereotypical reactions. In either case, the character will be a cliché: a second-hand creation, lazily constructed and dismissive of the reader's sensibilities. Characters need grease paint, but exaggerating their features beyond a certain point in the hope of making them more interesting or more easily identifiable can reduce the drama to pantomime, tragedy to farce.

Archetypes and stereotypes exist only in literature, never in life. Human beings are never as predictable as we think they are. The gap between expectation and result (in other words the narrative 'surprise') is the root of drama. If characters run along tramlines deviating neither to the left nor the right, not only will they be false, they will be boring. In fiction the gap between expectation and actuality is the source of much drama: 'will he/won't he' has been a story since the beginning of time.

Know your characters by knowing yourself

Vivid characters are born only when the writer knows them inside out. A good novelist is at least as much a psychologist as a wordsmith, for in the end, the depth and realness of your characters reflect your understanding of human beings.

True understanding of people comes about when we can see the world through their eyes, and feel their feelings as though they are our own. This quality of empathy is fundamental to the author's skill. Without it a novelist can create only flat characters. With limited empathy a novelist will have a limited range: to create only realistic characters of a certain type, namely people like the novelist.

How can we extend our range as writers, thinking ourselves inside the skin of a wide variety of characters? How could Shakespeare create Hamlet, Juliet, Lady Macbeth? Was he suffering from a multiple personality disorder? I doubt it. What he was doing was accessing the extraordinary resources available to him. Not his local library, but his *brain*.

The most complex structure in the known universe is the human brain: modern computers have hardly begun to approximate human brain functions, let alone intelligence. The human imaginative faculty is perhaps without bounds; it is certainly capable of inventing a cast of thousands. You think Shakespeare was different, that you don't have much of an imagination? Look at your dreams. You don't have dreams? I don't believe you.

Shakespeare didn't have to be mad to create King Lear, but he did have to engage with the part of himself that was a madman. Those who know of such things have said that King Lear is a convincing portrait of a psychotic breakdown. How did Shakespeare know? By visiting Bedlam, queuing up behind the other gawpers to laugh at the antics of the idiots? He may have, though I'm sure he didn't laugh. But more important than external research was the internal research, the visit to the part of him which is King Lear. And there is one part of us which can respond to everyone: madman, child, queen.

How to know your characters? Look inside: everything is there. All characters in fiction – like all characters in dreams – are parts of the writer, otherwise how could they be invented? They come from inside your head, nobody else's. *To know your characters, know yourself.*

> A writer's knowledge of himself, realistic and unromantic, is like a store of energy on which he must draw for a lifetime; one volt of it properly directed will bring a character alive.
>
> *Graham Greene*

Loving your characters

If you want to move people, you have to move yourself first. You must care about your characters in order for your readers to care about them. That means you should sympathize with them as well as empathize. You must have some sort of affection for your characters, particularly central characters, otherwise your disapproval will infect the story and your readers will be repulsed by them. Make your protagonists bad, by all means, fallible, two-faced and self-centred, but don't despise them.

If you can't bring yourself to like your characters, you must nevertheless love them. You must realize that under their characteristics, and regardless of their character, there is something else: their humanity. If you don't love them, you will always maintain a distance, and the reader will sense this.

> It seems to me important that you should always love the inner experience of the story, and the characters in it, experiencing along with them; rather than using them illustratively.
>
> *Malcolm Bradbury*

Roman à clef

Roman à clef is the convention of taking people from real life and disguising them in fiction. Strictly speaking, this reference to real life should be apparent to the reader, hence the name '*roman à clef*' ('novel with a key'), a novel containing a device for unlocking hidden meaning. An example is Aldous Huxley's novel, *Point Counter Point*, in which D. H. Lawrence, amongst others, is disguised. However, I use the term loosely to describe any appropriation of people from real life for use in fiction. There are advantages and disadvantages for the writer in this. The advantage is having a head start on the creative process: already you know something about your characters, perhaps a great deal.

The main problem is not, as many people think, the matter of libel. Even if people recognize themselves in your book (which is rare – few people see themselves as others do), they are probably more likely to feel flattered than offended. The disadvantage of taking characters from real life is that of finding yourself restricted when it comes to using your imagination. If your fictional creation has to do something which the real person wouldn't, you may find your characters refusing to do your bidding. A certain amount of pseudo-autonomy is a good sign; however, having your characters mutiny is rarely helpful in shaping a workable plot. The author must always be the boss – perhaps subordinate to the muse, but certainly in charge of the cast.

Use people from your life, by all means, but as a starting point, not as a model to copy. Many of my characters begin with a germ from real life, but then I allow them to develop along their own lines. Or I amalgamate characteristics from several people into one fictional creation.

> A useful trick is to look back upon a person with half-closed eyes, fully describing certain characteristics. A likeness isn't aimed at and couldn't be obtained, because a man's only himself amidst the particular circumstances of his life.
>
> *E. M. Forster*

The same restrictions apply to fictionalizing your own life. If the drama demands changes to the story, and you find yourself resistant to these changes because they didn't really happen, you may find yourself between two stools: fiction and autobiography.

Life is rarely as coherent as fiction with its beginning, middle and end. Even if it is, the fact that it really happened will only contribute to its appeal if the story is extraordinary. This is sometimes hard to gauge, particularly because our individual pasts are almost by definition interesting to us. What may seem significant to us may be trivial to the reader.

A writer, if he is any good, does not describe. He invents or *makes* out of knowledge personal and impersonal and sometimes he seems to have unexplained knowledge which could come from forgotten racial or family experience.

Ernest Hemingway

Things to try

1 Write a characterization list for your main cast. Cover both physical attributes and history. Include such things as: distinguishing features, style of dressing, the school they went to, siblings, type of upbringing, formative influences in childhood.

2 Interesting characters should have some type of internal conflict – the primary level of antagonism. What inner conflict could your protagonist have?

3 Idiosyncrasies and flaws help make characters more believable and often more sympathetic. What such qualities does your protagonist have?

4 In what ways are your protagonist's characterization and character at odds?

5 What character change, for good or bad, is in store for your main cast?

6 What forces are driving your main cast?

7 It is particularly at moments of stress (that is, when plot events are stacked up against a person, forcing then to make a critical choice) that we see a character's depth. Taking the following examples, write a character study for each in 300 words. Use at least three of the seven tools on page 55.

- An old woman is opening a letter from her son. He is suggesting she moves into a home for old people. She doesn't want to go.
- A businessman is late for work. He is stuck in a traffic jam.
- A young girl is driving a horse and cart late at night through rural lanes. She falls asleep and wakes with a start: the lamp has gone out and there has been an accident – the family horse has been killed by the shaft of another carriage.

(To see what Thomas Hardy does with the last of these examples, read Chapter 4 of *Tess of the d'Urbervilles*.)

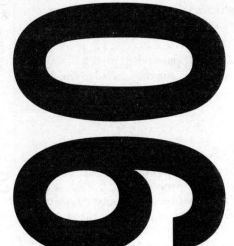

06
dialogue

In this chapter you will learn:
- about the three functions of speech and how to give the impression of real speech
- how to support dialogue
- about the three types of speech
- the conventions of written speech.

It is tempting to think that writing dialogue is the easiest part of fiction, but not so. Every word in a novel, including the dialogue, needs to do its work, otherwise it will begin to drag.

> The dialogue is generally the most agreeable part of a novel, but it is only so long as it tends in some way to the telling of the main story.
>
> *Anthony Trollope*

The trick of writing good dialogue is in giving the *impression* of real speech without emulating it. As life usually has no plot, so most conversations have no shape. Real speech is often repetitive, tautological and full of irrelevances: just try tape recording a conversation and then transcribing it. The result may be realistic, but it won't pass for the convention of 'slice of life' realism – it will probably be boring and far too long. An understandable temptation with beginners is to write a great deal of dialogue: it is often easy to do, and certainly more straightforward than the struggle most of us face with description and exposition. However, if you have too many interchanges or your speeches are too long, your reader's patience will be tested. The pleasure you find in writing dialogue must, after all, be shared by the reader in reading it. Good conversational speech may look easy, but it requires discipline and a firm editing hand.

Dialogue is like a rose bush – it often improves after pruning. I recommend you rewrite your dialogue until it is as brief as you can get it. This will mean making it quite unrealistically to the point. That is fine. Your readers don't want realistic speech, they want talk which spins the story along.

How to convey the sort of person who goes on and on, or talks for the sake of it? In other words, how to convey a bore? *Not* boringly. Do not replicate their speech, or your reader, like the targets of the bore's attention, will switch off. The paradox of the novelist is in making bores as fascinating as every other character. One way of achieving this is by showing other's reactions:

> Jack was talking about his car again, something about the wheel trims. Jill stifled a yawn.

Lose superfluous interactions. In a film this may go unnoticed, but on the page we are unconsciously looking for the significance of every utterance. If an interchange has no significance, we may become confused, thinking that we must be missing something.

The three functions of speech

Narrative speech should perform at least one of three functions.

1 Moving the story forwards

Sometimes the quickest, most important action comes out of our mouths. From the simple request or command to the most profound confession, speech is capable of fulfilling the first task of the fiction writer: telling the story.

2 Giving information

The imparting of information is an unavoidable necessity. We need to give credibility to the workings of the fictional world: how people got into a certain situation; how they can get out of it; the consequences of action; and so on. The problem is that sometimes this is boring stuff which can hold up the forward movement of the story. The giving of information should, therefore, be approached with sensitivity. Sometimes there is no option but to give an entire paragraph over to exposition. Often, however, we can disguise it in the action so that, like characterization, we need not absorb it all at once.

Using dialogue for exposition is legitimate, but beware of over-using it. If your characters are too obviously a mouthpiece for your intention, you will be guilty of what is called writing 'on the nose'. This means passages which read like stage directions or a cinematic voice-over. Suddenly your readers will see the artifice rather than the art, they will remember that it is a fiction they are reading, and the spell will be broken. Dialogue used for exposition often sounds hammy:

'When did we first meet, Carruthers?'

'Twenty years ago, old chap. The Summer of Love.'

'You were driving a pink VW, and I was hitch-hiking to see my girlfriend, now my wife – Anne.'

'It all comes back to me now. You were a student.'

'Eng. Lit. And you were a rookie journalist on *The Milwaukee Chronicle*.'

In cases like this it is better to cut your losses and use summary rather than pretend it is part of the drama:

> He met Carruthers 20 years ago in the Summer of Love. He was a student of English Literature, hitch-hiking to see his girlfriend, now his wife – Anne. Carruthers, a rookie journalist of *The Milwaukee Chronicle*, gave him a lift in his pink VW.

There is a saying amongst screenwriters: 'convert exposition to ammunition'. If you can sugar the pill by imparting information in a dramatic scene, your readers will hardly notice they are being informed. Thus, the two characters above could be rowing, and amid the insults, the necessary information could be inserted.

> 'You've been saying that for twenty years! I wish you'd never stopped your stupid pink VW to give a lift ...' (*et cetera*)

3 Contributing to characterization

This function should always be fulfilled, because every word that leaves your character's mouth will help illustrate the sort of person he or she is.

Giving the impression of real speech

As your characters have different physical and emotional characteristics, so too should they speak differently. A young man will use different vocabulary from his father; an English person and an Irish person of the same age and background will have different speech patterns and idioms; an aristocrat will not use the same language as a road sweep. Italians and French and Germans speak English in different ways; people from the North speak differently to their southern counterparts. It may be asking a lot, but by the end of the book, your readers should hopefully be capable of recognising the speakers without any clues other than their speech.

Real speech is often a chaotic affair involving interruptions, evasions, circumlocutions, poor grammar, bad language, silences, slang. Without exactly replicating these attributes, you need to indicate their existence. Very few people speak copybook English: your fictional creations should reflect this.

Dialect and foreign languages

The transcribing of dialect, complete with misspelt words and creative punctuation can be tedious for the reader. D. H. Lawrence occasionally used a full-blown form of dialect for his Nottinghamshire characters: 'Let me be mysen, and let me feel as if tha' wor littler than me! dunna ma'e me feel sma', an' down!', says Parkin in *John Thomas and Lady Jane*. We may very well want Parkin to be himself, but too much of this and he'll be doing it on his own.

The problem with transcribing dialect is not so much the vernacular, as the spelling. If readers have to puzzle over the meaning of a word, or even if the idiosyncratic spelling is just strange, their focus will stray from the scene to the artifice. If you want to establish a vernacular speaker you will probably find light touches are enough. If you use authentic speech patterns and local vocabulary, the occasional misspelt word will be enough to remind the reader of your character's origins. The purpose of dialogue, remember is to give the *impression* of realistic speech, not to replicate it.

Likewise, if your setting is in a non-English speaking country, the occasional foreign word – particularly one likely to be recognized by the average reader – is enough the remind us where we are. James Clavell's novel *Shogun* is a good example of this.

Sub-text

People in real life tend to fudge and hesitate, saying as much with what they don't say as with the words that leave their mouths. Very often – particularly in times of conflict – the words we speak only hint at what we mean. We have rows about the washing up, when in fact we are really arguing about our marriage. Therefore, be aware of the unspoken language, the sub-text of the dialogue. (I am reminded of the scene in Woody Allen's film *Annie Hall* in which subtitles of the true meaning of the spoken dialogue are flashed up.) If you want to make your scenes more psychologically complex and more accurately reflect the essence of real speech, be aware of the undercurrents of meaning.

Supporting your dialogue

Meaning is not only a matter of the words we say, but the way we say them. Sometimes bald speech needs assistance:

> 'I love you,' he said from behind his newspaper.
> 'Really?'
> 'Yes.'

This says a certain amount, although it doesn't tell us how seriously the man intends his words to be taken. Although speech can happily stand alone, sometimes it requires support in order to bring out its full meaning. Supporting the same words of dialogue with abstract explanation goes some way to putting flesh on the bones of meaning:

> 'I love you,' he said from behind his newspaper.
> 'Really?'
> 'Yes.' He really *did* love her.

The most effective way of supporting your dialogue is often by giving physical clues to the meaning, for instance:

> 'I love you,' he said from behind his newspaper.
> 'Really?'
> He lowered the paper and held her gaze for a second. 'Yes.'

A picture is sometimes worth a thousand words. Using dialogue in conjunction with carefully chosen action is the simplest and most effective technique I know, making previously inert scenes come to life.

Physical action performs three functions: it helps break up the dialogue (important if you have a whole page of it); it anchors the speech in the scene (reminding us where we are and what our characters are doing); and perhaps most importantly, contributes to characterization. The action which contributes the most is revealing action, rather than action for the sake of it.

Well-chosen action will say something about your characters, hopefully identifying them as nothing else does. A woman who drums her carefully painted fingernails while waiting for someone to pick up the phone; a young man who can't meet the eyes of the person he is speaking to; the old woman who unconsciously plucks at the bedclothes while listening to the doctor – pictures, all.

Types of speech

There are three types of speech:

- direct
- indirect or reported
- interiors.

For example:

> 'I wish you would leave me alone, Jack'

is direct: this is audible speech, and conventionally appears between speech marks.

> Jill told Jack she wished he would leave her alone

is indirect speech, reported as though by an onlooker.

> I wish you would leave me alone, Jack, Jill thought

is called an interior or a monologue. Here we are eavesdropping on her thoughts, although no words leave her mouth. There is no technical difficulty in the use of interiors – it is the same as direct speech, minus the speech marks. If it is unclear, you can add 'she thought' after the thought, although this is not always necessary.

The value of interiors is to give the reader another level of insight into character. For instance:

> 'Are you doing anything after work?' Jack asked, leaning across her desk.
>
> Jill tried to smile, but she could smell cigarette smoke on his breath. I wish you would leave me alone, Jack, she thought.
>
> 'Not particularly,' she said, edging away.

He said/she said, and attributive verbs

We don't read every word on the page, but scan them, often not bothering to read the end of a sentence if we have already captured the meaning. This doesn't mean that as writers we can afford to be lax, but it does mean that there are blind spots on the page. One of those is 'he said/she said'. Don't worry if you are the type of writer who feels most comfortable attributing each piece of speech. To continue with Jack and the reluctant Jill:

> 'How about coming out with me?' he said.
> 'Well ...' she said.
> 'We could go for a meal,' he said.
> 'I'm on a diet,' she said.
> 'How about a drink then?' he said.
> 'Jack?' she said.
> 'Yes?' he said.
> 'Leave me alone!' she said.

With dialogue as bald as this you might be pushing your luck a bit; however, filling in this dialogue with supportive action, few readers would notice the he said/she said refrain.

Some writers like to leave dialogue unattributed, and this is fine if it is very clear who is speaking, as in the above example. In long interchanges, particularly if the content doesn't clearly indicate who is speaking, or if more than two people are speaking, readers may find themselves having to count back. In this case an occasional indicator would be enough.

The most common problem for the reader is not a lack of information, but a surfeit of it. If you insist on attributive verbs for each piece of speech, your reader will watch fascinated as you climb further and further out along a branch which is bound to snap. For instance:

'How about coming out with me?' Jack asked.
'Well ...' Jill hesitated.
'We could go for a meal,' he proffered.
'I'm on a diet,' she lied.
'How about a drink then?' he suggested.
'Jack?' she growled.
'Yes?' he grinned.
'Leave me alone!' she snapped.

Attributive verbs have the effect of taking the eye away from the speech. In effect, we check that our reading is correct. Sometimes the attributive verb is superfluous, for example 'he suggested' after 'How about a drink then?' is a waste of a reader's attention (a minor point perhaps, but that's what a novel is – a collection of minor points). Sometimes detail corrals our imagination in unnecessary ways: you might have trouble imagining Jill growling 'Jack': in your mind she might have groaned it, in which case you would have to adjust your interpretation when you read 'growled'. Sometimes in your quest for variety of attributive verbs, you will get plain silly and find yourself using archaisms such as 'expostulated', 'ejaculated', 'exclaimed', 'cried', when you just mean 'said'.

The only time an attributive verbs pulls its weight is when the meaning or delivery of the spoken words isn't clear from the words themselves. For instance, in the above example 'she lied' is necessary for us to fully understand her intent.

Outer and inner ears

In order to test your dialogue, try speaking it aloud – or better still, have someone else read it to you, preferably someone who isn't a consummate actor. If the reader wrestles with the syntax or the idiom, take note. Just because it comes out easily in the writing doesn't mean it reads well.

> Each phrase of each sentence, like an air or a recitative in music, should be so artfully compounded out of long and short, out of accented and unaccented, as to gratify the sensual ear. And of this the ear is the sole judge. It is impossible to lay down laws.
>
> *Robert Louis Stevenson*

Although reading aloud can be of help, it is the inner ear rather than the 'sensual' one which must have the casting vote. Few readers will read your dialogue aloud; in the end it must work in the silence of their mind or not at all.

Conventions of written speech

There are no rules for the layout of speech: writers from James Joyce to Malcolm Bradbury have used their own form. However, the modern convention is:

- use single speech marks
- a new paragraph is required every time a new speaker talks, even if it is just one word
- any action associated with the speaker which immediately precedes or follows them speaking is in the same paragraph.

Things to try

1 Tape record two or more people talking and then transcribe it. Now rewrite it, editing it down and using supportive action. Look at both drafts: which is more interesting? Which more accurately conveys the 'truth' of the situation?

2 Write a scene of people disagreeing with each other, in 300 words using mainly dialogue. If you have a novel in progress, use the characters from the story (even if the scene is to be abandoned in the final draft). If you have nothing to get you going, try one of the following:

- Some money has gone missing at a bank. The manager is interviewing all the clerks one by one in his office. Although holding back from an explicit accusation, the manager suspects one person in particular. The clerk is defensive and indignant, but also intimidated by the manager.
- There has been a three-way collision between cars on the road. One person is clearly at fault and denying it. Another person is unsure whose fault it is, but just to make sure, blames somebody else. The third person is innocent, but shaken by the accident.
- A young couple are having a first date in a restaurant. They are trying not to spoil the evening, but they disagree about everything they talk about.

3 Look at your dialogue either in the above exercise, or in your novel in progress: do the characters speak distinctly, using their own vocabulary and speech patterns, or do they all speak the same?

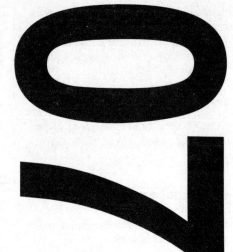

07

viewpoint

In this chapter you will learn:
- the advantages and disadvantages of the four types of viewpoint used in fiction writing
- about when to use the present and past tenses
- about the impact of writing from different character viewpoints
- about tone, the quality of language used in writing.

A novelist is like a film director. It is not enough to say: in this scene such-and-such happens to so-and-so. If that were the case you would produce a long synopsis, which in film is called a *treatment*, instead of a dramatic narrative. The novelist and film director must decide *how* to portray such-and-such happening to so-and-so. Of the technical resources available to the director, the most important is the camera. The director cannot film everything from every angle – he or she must make decisions: where to place the camera; what angles to film from; what to film; what to leave out. The writer, likewise, must decide where to position the novelistic camera. This is what is meant by 'viewpoint'.

> The choice of the point(s) of view from which the story is told is arguably the most important single decision that the novelist has to make, for it fundamentally affects the way readers will respond, emotionally and morally, to the fictional characters and their actions.
>
> *David Lodge*

In a murder mystery, are you going to tell the story from the detective's viewpoint, or the suspect's or the murderer's? Or a combination of all three? Alfred Hitchcock denied us the murderer's viewpoint to famous effect in his film *Psycho*. The effect would have been very different if he hadn't done so: much of the suspense would have been dissipated, and all of the mystery. Some novels bring to the fore the significance of different perspectives. John Fowles' first novel, *The Collector*, was the story of an abduction told from two viewpoints – the kidnapper and the victim. The same story, but different camera angles.

If the viewpoint decision is the most important decision to make, it can also be the most complex. That is, unless you have proceeded intuitively, for more often than not the viewpoint decision will make itself even before the first word is written. Especially if you have a clearly defined central character and a feel for the book, there is often little hesitation.

There is a lot to be said for intuition: a novel is far too complex – infinitely so, I believe – to be fully approachable through reasoned argument. However, if you are aware of friction in the early stages of telling your story, it could be because you have chosen the wrong viewpoint. In which case it is worth a certain amount of examination of the options and their respective advantages.

Two questions

Before we move on to examine the types of viewpoint, it is useful to ask two questions, not that they will necessarily solve the problem, but they could point us in the right direction. The questions are: Whose story is it? and What is the theme?

Whose story is it?

Is there a single hero, or more than one? If there are several, who is more important? Are they equally important? The word 'hero' is misleading here, implying qualities which the lead character may not have, for instance the unnamed narrator in Daphne du Maurier's *Rebecca* is far from heroic. But so too is the word 'protagonist' misleading, for sometimes the 'first actor' is not the main player; however, they are the main focus for the impact of the action. Thus a young child could be the protagonist of a story about his parent's divorce.

There are three types of protagonist, three options for choosing who is to be the main focus of the story. In descending order of occurrence:

The single protagonist

This is the simplest option for the writer and reader alike. There is no difficulty identifying the hero.

Dual protagonists

This is a little trickier; you have two characters with more or less equal weight. As their author, you must decide who gets the spotlight when they are on stage together, whose action to follow when they are apart.

Multiple protagonists

This is the trickiest of the three. Few novelists try this, because lacking a character focus, the story itself could lack focus. Joseph Conrad used this form in *The Nigger of the Narcissus*.

If you have more than one protagonist, they should ideally be intimately connected, that is:

- be in a relationship together, or
- have their fates bound together, or
- face a common source of conflict.

In other words, though distinct in themselves, they should share a common quest. Some stories involving more than one protagonist will share all three of these, for instance *Romeo and Juliet*. If there is not a common goal it may split the book down the middle, in which case you may need to decrease the significance of one of them and turn it into a subplot.

What is the theme?

Theme will be explored more fully in Chapter 10. Briefly, 'theme' is the meaning behind the action – what the author is saying about the subject. For instance, if the subject is a marital break up due to adultery, the theme could be 'love is more important than commitment'. If this was the case, the viewpoint character is likely to be the adulterous partner. If the theme was 'loyalty is more important that attraction', then the point of view of the cuckold may be the more obvious choice.

Types of viewpoint

In fiction there are four available options, each with its own advantages and disadvantages.

First person viewpoint

Sometimes called 'intense' viewpoint, this is when all the action is seen through a single 'I'. There is only one camera, as it were, and it looks through the eyes of a single person – the protagonist. This means only action that the protagonist witnesses can be reported. It is easy to hold a novel within such a tight framework – the viewpoint doesn't get out of hand because it is very simple.

The first person viewpoint has more intrinsic dramatic focus than the other options. Because the reader lives, as it were, inside the character, this option is capable of a singleness of impact, hence 'intense' viewpoint. Because of this, it lends itself well to a very intimate treatment, which is useful if the subject is a personal, internal process.

Because the readers can know only what the protagonist knows, it is easy for the author to spring surprises on them. Suspense and tension, therefore, often work well with a first person viewpoint.

Another advantage accrues because there is no need for the author to deliberately withhold information – what you see is what you get. (Unless the narrator is unreliable, as in Agatha Christie's *The Murder of Roger Ackroyd*, a murder mystery in which it transpires the culprit is the narrator himself. Unreliable narrators are a neat trick perhaps, but the author is open to accusations of unsporting deviousness.)

The first person viewpoint in the most straightforward option. Having a wider focus will increase the number of decisions the author has to make: should I tell the reader what is happening in the next room, what so-and-so is thinking? The disadvantages are the opposite of the advantages. Nothing can happen without the viewpoint character knowing about it. It may be simple, but it is restrictive. If you have a very complicated story, you will have to have a lot of people coming in with messages, or an abundance of phone calls and letters.

Is it possible to have more than one first person narrator? John Fowles succeeded with it in *The Collector*; however, it was necessary to divide the novel into parts. An ambitious thing to do – good luck if you want to try it.

If you write in the first person, and if the narrator bears even a passing similarity to you, don't be surprised if people think it's autobiographical. Proceeding in the knowledge of this might require some courage on your behalf!

Third person viewpoint

This is probably the most common convention: stories concerning 'he' and 'she'. There are two ways you can tell a third person story: a single viewpoint or a multiple viewpoint.

The single viewpoint

This has the same technical advantages and disadvantages of a first person single viewpoint: the main difference is the pronoun. The third person is perhaps less intimate, less confessional. This may be a plus if you want to avoid self-pity or self-indulgence in your protagonist. If you have a sad story to tell and you relate it from the viewpoint of the person it happened to, an unsympathetic reader could hear it as the whining of a victim. Tell the same story in the third person, and the effect may be one of pathos. The exception is if the narrator has no self-pity: a rare thing indeed. My second novel, *Billy Bayswater*, began its life in the third person. The first draft read:

> Billy had something wrong with his brain. He touched his face in the mirror and smiled. "Billy Bayswater brain,' he said.

Although the work was going well, by the time a week had passed I could smell burning rubber. There was a handbrake on somewhere – I could sense the resistance. I realized that I was holding Billy at bay, not allowing myself to get too close, in part because I wanted to tell a tragic story without being maudlin. (The other part was because an intense viewpoint cuts both ways – this was going to be painful if I got too involved.) I thought I would try it in first person:

> Billy's got summat wrong with his brain – that's what they say. I touch my face in the mirror and smile. Billy Bayswater brain.

Suddenly the story came alive. Not only was I inside his skin, but I could use his language; and because of his lack of awareness, there was no danger of self-pity. Intimacy of this type is often central to the appeal of a novel: imagine Catcher in the Rye written in the third person – I'm sure it would lose a lot.

When choosing a single viewpoint – whether first person or third person – it is important to select a character whom you can easily inhabit. In order to make the character credible and authoritative, you will need to be privy to his or her thoughts, seeing the world through your character's eyes. Although it is important to know all your main characters well, you should know your viewpoint character inside out. This doesn't mean you need to share the same gender or history. My first novel was written through the eyes of a woman, my second through the eyes of an adolescent epileptic; however, you should be capable of imagining yourself within their skin.

The third person multiple viewpoint
This is when the film director, as it were, has more than one camera at his or her disposal. Now the director can film anything: events happening in different locations, even if they happen at the same time. However, now the director needs to hire a good editor, for important decisions need to be made about whose viewpoint to follow.

To use multiple viewpoint well requires discipline. Having open season can be disorienting for the reader. For instance:

As he opened the door he glanced at his wife. Oh hell, he thought when he saw her face. I'm in trouble again. 'Good morning, darling,' he smiled. She might forgive me if I'm nice to her, he thought.

She said nothing, just watched him as he crossed the kitchen. He was unsteady on his feet and caught his thigh on the corner of the table. She saw his jaw tighten. It must have hurt, but he kept quiet. He feels guilty, she thought. Good.

He could feel her disapproving glare like a sunlamp on his back as he poured out his coffee. Nice and strong, he put in extra sugar to clear his hangover. He had ten minutes to get to work. Please God, don't let her row with me.

She listened to the clinking of the spoon against the china mug. She didn't know whether she hated him or just despised him. He had promised to be home early. *Promised*.

The viewpoint here goes: husband, wife, husband, wife. If you bat viewpoint backwards and forwards like a ball, the reader get dizzy. We would rather live in one head at a time, guessing, if necessary, what the other person is thinking. It is best to decide whose scene it is going to be, and then stick to your decision. Again, this may be an intuitive decision, but if you are still unsure, look at the point of the scene. In this case, which is more important to convey – the husband's guilty feelings or the wife's anger?

If the scene is long, you can get away with swapping once, or if one of the characters exits, transfer the point of view to the other. Here, for instance, we could have focussed on the husband as he burns his mouth on his coffee in his hurry to leave, and then paid attention to the wife as she sits at the table thinking things over.

A straightforward way to combine viewpoints is chapter by chapter, which is what Mario Puzo did in *The Godfather*. The change of viewpoint will still be noticed, but the join between them will be legitimized by the gear change of a fresh chapter.

If you choose multiple viewpoints, limit the numbers you afford it to, perhaps just the protagonist and one or two others. If you include minor characters – the taxi driver, the waiter, the woman on the bus – you could lose focus to such an extent that the story becomes fuzzy. There is only a certain amount of room on the stage (to change my image to a theatrical one): having actors jostling for attention will seem chaotic.

The advantage of shifting viewpoint is an expanded panoramic vision. This is fine, but only as long as the author isn't caught at it. If the reader notices the shift in viewpoint, or even worse, is confused about who 'you' refers to (the second person 'you' is called a 'shifter' in linguistics; that is, a designation which changes according to who the speaker is) awareness of the author will intrude in the reading process. This is like the moment in a bad film (back to my original image) when the boom microphone bobs into view. Such reflexiveness can be intentional, in which case we are in the realm of metafiction, that is, fiction about fiction. But that is straying far from the classic novel which is the subject of this book.

God's eye view

This is multiple viewpoint taken as far as it can go. A truly omniscient viewpoint hovers above the story, the reader listening in to character's thoughts like a telepathic eavesdropper. The advantage is manifest: nothing is hidden, the fictional world is laid out in front of us like a map.

In some novels the divine status is less exalted, and we have a sort of demi-god's eye view where the deity makes occasional visits to the lower worlds, appearing in the guise of a narrator in a single viewpoint story. For instance, a chapter could begin like this:

> The early morning sun shone as brightly and as sweetly as a Disney cartoon on Peewee's house. The white slats of the picket fence against the perfect green of the lawn was a picture to behold. A blackbird bobbed its tail and opened its throat to sing. The postman, a parcel under his arm, whistled happily as he knocked on the front door.

and then move onto a single viewpoint in the next paragraph:

> Peewee heard the postman's knock and sat up straight. Today's the day, he thought. He leapt from his bed and banged on the window frame to open it, but it was stuck. He could see the postman by the front door. 'I'm here,' he called. 'Yoo-hoo.' He banged harder on the frame and heard the pane crack.

continuing with the single viewpoint unless or until the narrator is needed again.

The disadvantage of a god's eye view is significant: the reader, like the narrator, can float above the scene, passing through walls like a ghost, never really getting involved. If your intention is to produce a cool, perhaps ironic tone, this distance may be in your favour. If you have an emotional tale to tell you may find the effect is the opposite of intense.

What tense?

Basically, there are two main options: present tense and past tense. It is more usual to tell stories in the past tense, a tradition which perhaps goes back to the days when story tellers related tales of a mythical past.

The advantage the present tense has over the past tense is in giving a sense of immediacy. When I changed viewpoint in *Billy Bayswater*, I also changed the tense from past to present, with the intention of increasing the closeness between the reader's world and Billy's.

The impact of viewpoint decisions

The only rule about the use of viewpoint and tense is that there *is* no rule. If a particular technique works, use it. Some successful novelists are cavalier with viewpoint, dealing it out like a pack of playing cards, some remain with a single focus. It is important to realize there is nothing inferior about using the single viewpoint: a simple form is not an inferior form. Nor does a sophisticated treatment or use of tenses ensure a good book. In the end, everything should be justifiable in terms of plot, because otherwise, why do it?

This is complicated stuff, and is where reading plenty of fiction can be useful. Read critically, seeing how the author uses technique, and what effect is achieved.

Compare the impact of these scenes, both describing parents leaving a young son at boarding school. The first is from *The Prodigy*, Herman Hesse's second novel:

> When the time came round for the boys to say goodbye to their mothers and father, it was a much sadder business. Some on foot, some by coach, some in any kind of transport they had been able to find in their haste were now disappearing from the view of their abandoned offspring and continued to wave their handkerchiefs for a long time in the mild September air until the forest finally swallowed up the travellers and their sons returned quiet and thoughtful to the monastery.

This is a third person adult's viewpoint (in fact, a god's eye view). James Joyce's second novel, *A Portrait of the Artist as a Young Man*, published nine years later, deals with a similar scene in this way:

> The first day in the hall of the castle when she had said goodbye she had put up her veil double to her nose to kiss him: and her nose and eyes were red. But he had pretended not to see that she was going to cry. She was a nice mother but she was not so nice when she cried. And his father had given him two fiveshilling pieces for pocket money. And his father had told him if he wanted anything to write home to him and, whatever he did, never peach on a fellow.

Joyce takes the child's viewpoint, focussing on the details that a child would. What impact does this have? Suddenly the tripod of our figurative camera is lowered: we see the world from the level of a child while Herman Hesse's camera is on the top of a crane. With Joyce, we have a human scale (and importantly, a *small* human's scale), in the Hesse example, a more considered, philosophical attitude. Which is more effective? Though critical theory is never more than a matter of opinion, I consider that the passage from Joyce is both stronger and weaker than Hesse's. Stronger, because if our protagonist is a youngster, viewing the world as an adult reduces some of the vividness of the telling. The detail Joyce chooses to give us (the red nose and pocket money) contributes more to the creation of a live character than Hesse's focussing on modes of transport.

Herman Hesse, however, has the advantage of using the more simple, and therefore more forceful tense. While Hesse says 'When the time came round ...', Joyce, to be consistent would have said "When the time *had come* round ...' While Joyce says 'when she *had said* goodbye she *had put* up her veil', Hesse would have said 'when she said goodbye she put up her veil'. Does this quibbling about tenses show an unnecessary pickiness towards the work of a great master? Perhaps. However, it is my opinion we should lose all superfluous words, streamlining our prose so the readers forget they are deciphering a semiotic convention. We have to somehow condition the reader's synapses so the words on the page seem as though they have come from the reader's head, not ours.

Tone

As well as viewpoint, there is something we can call 'tone', that is, the quality of language the writer uses. This, in its own way, has as much impact on the reader's experience as does viewpoint. To return to the image of the film director with a camera, the choice of tone is akin to the choice of filter on the lens and how the scene is lit. Is the picture to be distorted? Softened round the edges? Shown starkly, under a bright light? Although there are no clear distinctions between soft and stark, straight and distorted, there are obvious extremes of tone which, as E. M. Forster suggested, we can call Impersonal and Personal. Impersonal language is more formal, and remains largely uncoloured by the viewpoint character, while the Personal tone is more conversational, using the vocabulary and idiom of speech. A second advantage of Joyce choosing the child's viewpoint is the privileged personal tone it allows him to use. A sentence such as 'She was a nice mother but she was not so nice when she cried' would have been incongruous and twee had we not been seeing the action through the eyes of a child. As it is, it contributes to our inhabiting the mind of a child – clearly Joyce's intention.

Taken to the extreme, the personal tone can become a so-called 'stream of consciousness', a style of writing that James Joyce also used to famous effect. Compare these scenes set in graveyards; the first is from my novel, *The Life Game*:

> It was late August and the Atlantic wind flattened the uncut couch grass on the bare hillside. It was a bleak spot for a graveyard, on an exposed slope facing the reek, a triangle of Clew Bay visible in the tuck between two mountains. There was no church or building of any sort, just a drystone wall to keep the sheep out and the incongruous tombstones like granite outcrops ... Kate wandered through the graveyard while Michael tidied up his wife's grave. Brushing aside the weeds and scraping off the moss she read the inscriptions. *Here lies the body of Patrick McGuinn; Pray for the soul of Mary Grady*.

The second extract is from James Joyce's *Ulysses*:

> Mr Bloom walked unheeded along his grove by saddened angels, crosses, broken pillars, family vaults, stone hopes praying with upcast eyes, old Ireland's hearts and hands. More sensible to spend the money on some charity for the living. Pray for the repose of the soul of. Does anybody really? Plant him and have done with him. Like down a coalshoot. Then lump them together to save time. All soul's day. Twentyseventh I'll be at his grave. Ten shillings for the gardener. He keeps it free of weeds.

Both scenes are similarly related in the third person, past tense. The tones, however, are very different. There is no intrinsic advantage in being either personal or impersonal, the success of a tone depending as it does, on its appropriateness to what the author is trying to do. The fashion of contemporary literature – perhaps all culture – is towards the informal; the modern novelist, certainly, is less distant, more of a buddy and less of a tutor than in formal times. But why do some novelists choose a highly personal tone? The most compelling reason is because using the language of the protagonist, particularly one who holds nothing back from readers, means we can be more intimate with them. An impersonal tone will hold the reader at bay, which indeed, may be an advantage if pathos or irony is intended.

There is no right and wrong in this, just a matter of choosing the most effective tools for the job. Perhaps as novelists we need to feel our way into these questions, allowing our narrative decisions to make themselves. Perhaps we should examine our choices only if we suspect we're using a hammer when a screwdriver would be better.

Things to try

1 Take a piece of your own writing and rewrite it in
   (a) a different viewpoint
   (b) a different tense.

2 Take a passage from a favourite novel and rewrite it, changing viewpoint and tense. Assess the impact of the change.

3 Relate one of the following scenes in 300 words, first from one viewpoint, and then from another:

   • The first day at school. A young teacher, fresh from college, faces his or her first class. (The viewpoint of the teacher, and then one of the pupils.)

   • There has been a road crash. (Viewpoint of a by-stander, and then the crash victim.)

   • A young woman helps an old blind man across the road. (Viewpoint of the woman, and then the man.)

   Now relate the same scene through the God's eye view.

setting the scene

In this chapter you will learn:
- about researching and choosing the setting for your story
- how to make a scene real, visualizing it in your mind and using the words and names to paint the picture on paper
- to focus on what is important, unique and special about the person, room or landscape you are writing about.

Characters and their actions need to be anchored in some sort of physical reality, otherwise they will lack a sense of substance. In our fascination and excitement for the unfolding drama, we may underestimate the importance of setting. The setting of a novel is like the flour in a cake: perhaps less compelling than the nuts and dried fruit, but if you forget to include flour in the recipe, you'll have no cake.

Sometimes a sense of place will be so subtle as not to be noticed; sometimes it will dominate the story, for instance Egdon Heath in Hardy's *Return of the Native*, or the labour camp in Solzhenitsyn's *One Day in the Life of Ivan Denisovitch*, or the pink house in Styron's *Sophie's Choice*. But whether to the fore or not, a place should have a character as much as any of the cast. And like human characters, it has the same requirements of realness: a sense of three dimensions, credibility, and the feeling that the author is speaking from experience.

Researching the setting

> The author must know his countryside, whether real or imagined, like his hand.
>
> *Robert Louis Stevenson*

If your setting is familiar to you, there is the advantage that you won't have much research to do. If you don't know the physical world of your story, you need to get to know it. Real places can be visited, or if that's not possible, read about. Use any resource you can: watch movies which were filmed there, talk to people who know the setting well, read guide books, study street plans. If you can go there, don't just look at the big picture, but notice the small things: smells, the type of litter, the look of the people who live there. If it is a building, notice the quality of the light, how the floorboards squeak underfoot, or the strip light in the kitchen buzzes. If it is a foreign country absorb as much of it as you can: the quality of the bank notes (in Pakistan they are often so old, they are as soft as cloth), how people drink their tea (quarter of an inch of sugar in the bottom in Turkey, and the spoon still in the glass) the telephone dialling tones, the taste of the water and quality of plumbing. It is the small things which can make all the difference in evoking the atmosphere of a place.

If your setting is imaginary, you need to be able to answer exactly the same sorts of questions. Just as you will be able to fully know your characters only when you have fully imagined them, so too must you know the place well enough in order to answer *any* question about it. Not that you will have the information to hand, but that, if necessary, your intuition will supply it. The research in this case is internal – you must let your imagination go to work. The advantage? Cheap on the pocket and because the place is not real, nobody can contradict you. The disadvantage? If your imagining is not thorough, it won't seem real anyway.

Once again, there is a difference between information and truth. A certain veracity is needed, but the essence of a setting is far more important. A reader who doesn't know the setting will probably take your word for the information, and unless you make a significant blunder, those who do know it will fill in the missing bits without being aware of it. However, if you fail to capture the truth of a place both types of reader will sense something amiss.

The reader should have no trouble seeing the backdrop behind the action. Whether actual or imagined, in order to effectively communicate this sense of place, requires the author to view it *outside in*. This means seeing it as the reader might, particularly someone for whom the setting is unfamiliar. See it freshly, without prejudice or a dull eye: this advice holds true for all physical description, whether of people or places. Your setting doesn't have to be magnificent or exotic – it could be a council house, or an office – but it should be *special*. It should have a presence to it. Powerful artists are those who often show us familiar things in unfamiliar ways, helping us see through our self-imposed blinkers to the specialness, the uniqueness of the place.

> The novelist's job is to reveal and unfold, not simply portray. The novelist works with the things that pass unobserved by others, captures them in motion, brings them out into the open.
>
> *Joao Guimaraes Rosa*

Choosing your setting

Sometimes your setting will choose itself. If this is the case, don't resist the pull, that is, unless the choice of location stretches the reader's credibility. If you are casting around for a suitable setting, consider what different places offer in terms of dramatic resources. I have found two things in particular of great value: isolation (not being able to run for help enables the pressure to mount), and weather (particularly extremes). Although everywhere has dramatic potential, some landscapes lend themselves more than others to fictionalization: isolated cottages, windswept fishing villages, big cities. Would *Wuthering Heights* have been as powerful set in a city; *The Heart of Darkness* in Surrey and not Africa?

Making scenes real

Experience is not an abstract matter; it is deeply rooted in our physicality. When we think of a place we know, we don't see 'room', 'building', 'scenery' – these are concepts. We see the flowered wallpaper, the mullion windows and varnished front door, the sweep of a hill. When we look back at events in our pasts we may label them: 'my first day at school', 'the time I fell off my bike', but if we look closer, we realize what made them real at the time, and what makes them real now is the sight and sound and feel of things. Experiences are concrete, tangible, sensory – it is only later that we conceptualize them.

> People's minds are changed through observation and not through argument.
>
> *Will Rogers*

One way of looking at the novelist's task is as a changer of minds. The change being sought may be profound, or it may be just a change from boredom to excitement, but just as the protagonist should be different by the end of the tale, so too should the reader. How to change a reader's mind? By argument, discussion, persuasion? This may have a place in the novel, but the starting point is far closer to home. The novelist must begin by painting a sufficiently vivid picture of an imaginative world which is capable of firing the reader's imagination. How to paint such a picture? The first step in making it real for yourself.

Recreate a scene, don't describe it

Your reader will experience the reality of a setting only if you have experienced it for yourself, even if only in your imagination. If you are writing about your first day at school, you need to return there in your memory and see the red plastic chairs, and smell the Plasticine and gravy, and hear the sound of a boy crying for his mother. Revisiting the past may be uncomfortable, but if you want a setting with depth, you need to go into the discomfort. Recreate a scene, don't describe it. Inhabit it, don't write around it. Once you have set the scene in your own mind, *then* you can be more conceptual, talking about your feelings and the thoughts you were having. Only then will words like 'classroom', 'afraid', 'why is that boy crying?' really hit home with the reader.

What the reader is seeking to do is vicariously experience what you are evoking: excitement in a thriller, romance in a love story; and tangibility in terms of the setting. If you want to communicate this experience fully, the readers will, in effect, have to sit in the red plastic chair with you. This means supplying them with sensory clues so they can make it real for themselves. As simple as that.

We can't communicate something which the readers haven't already experienced. Try describing 'blue' to a blind person. The way verbal communication works is by supplying clues which set off a process within readers, in effect reminding them of something they have already experienced. In this way, they will be able to think themselves into your skin because they will compare your experience with something similar to their own. Even if we've never sat in a red plastic chair, most of us know 'red', 'plastic' and 'chair'.

The importance of detail

Storytelling is picture painting with words. This means authors need to keep their eyes open and convey what they see. And once conveyed, to step back, to withhold judgement. An author just gives the facts in all their specificity and concreteness – what the Zen poetess Natalie Goldberg calls 'original detail', that is, the unadorned, humble facts – and allows the readers to reach their own conclusions. Trust the power of images to evoke.

> Stay with what is and it will give you everything that isn't. From this wooden table I am leaning on, I can build a whole world of fiction.
>
> *Natalie Goldberg*

The importance of names

A novelist should be omniscient. You should know your creation as a little God would – all the detail, all the depths. And the most specific way of indicating something is by naming it. So use the names of things: say 'elm', not 'tree'; 'angora', not 'wool'. You need to be informed, so if necessary learn the names of plants and flowers, breeds of dog, tones of colour, types of cloud, brands of cigarette.

Naming helps you and the reader get a grasp of things, it helps anchor you on the page. And it tells the reader something of vital importance: that the author is authoritative. The absence of detail, the failure to name something betrays a lack of grasp of the subject. Use of detail, on the other hand, says 'I was there and it was like this'. When detail is absent, the reader senses that the author is likewise absent. When the author is removed from the page it is like speaking to someone behind a wall: we can hear the words, but they're muffled. We have to guess the expression on the speaker's face, the emphasis they are giving words. We get the gist, but the spirit is lacking.

Perception and selection

Perception is the first step: what is really happening, not what you think is happening. What is the real physical tangible reality? As the motto goes: show, don't tell. But just 'showing' isn't enough, in the same way that a film director just waving the camera blindly around isn't enough. The art is in the selecting, the editing, the discrimination. When you are describing a scene, *choose*. Focus on what is important, unique, special (everything is important, but there is a hierarchy of significance) about this person, this room, this landscape.

There is no checklist against which to measure your decisions: *this* is what it means to be an artist – the use of aesthetic judgement to choose between what is live and what is inert.

> The only classification of the novel I can understand is into that which has life and that which has not.
>
> *Henry James*

Some objects are inexplicably 'alive', seemingly vibrating with character; others are dead, lacking energy and the ability to assert themselves on the scene. D. H. Lawrence called this quality of aliveness, 'quickness', which he gropingly defined as 'an odd sort of fluid, changing, grotesque or beautiful relatedness'. We live in a world in which objects are increasingly dead: mass-produced consumer items, synthetic material, throw-away gimmicks and junk – it is your job to sift through this to find the 'quick'.

What to show and what to leave out

How much information to give is often a problem at first, but once you get the hang of it, you'll probably find it easy. I find it useful to think of it as a film: what would I expect/want to see on the screen? You don't have to show everything – allow the readers to fill in the missing bits for themselves. They have an imagination as well as you.

Respect the reader's intelligence as well. There is no need to cross every 't' and dot every 'i'. The average reader can reach his or her own conclusion, deciding what is significant and what is not. If you create vivid enough scenery, your readers will move your characters around it for you, but only if you leave the readers with room for their imaginations to breathe. It's better to give too little than too much.

Visualization

Hopefully you are capable of visualizing the scene so vividly that you can look around in your mind's eye and select any detail you want. Don't worry if you don't have this facility at the moment – it improves with practice. It helps if you take your time: a novelist needs to take things slowly, not rushing ahead. If I have trouble visualising a scene, I try again just before I fall asleep at night, or when I'm in the bath, or feeling drowsy in the afternoon. If the imagination has stage fright, try relaxing, taking the pressure off. We have extraordinary imaginations, and truly marvellous abilities to evoke pictures in our minds. All of us.

Close your eyes and get as much of a picture as you can; then try running the action as though it's a film. Once you have a picture in mind, describe what you see – the subtle things as well as the obvious – as simply and as accurately as you can.

When I come across passages of 'telling' I sometimes feel that the author is struggling to picture the scene. This isn't a lack of talent showing, just a lack of visualization. A shame, because this is the most fun part of writing. What other job can you do with your eyes closed and your feet up?

Seeing imaginary scenes with your eyes closed (or open, if that is the case), and then transcribing them onto paper is a large part of the writer's job. Why is sight so important? Because the impact of settings in real life is largely visual (about half of the brain is given over to visual processing, so they say). Humans are very visually oriented, so giving visual clues to the reader is important. If we were bats, our books would be full of sound pictures.

The importance of focal length

Unless you focus your own eye well, everything might seem a blur to the reader. Ford Madox Ford recommended seeing the action you are describing as taking place on a brightly lit stage – everything is available for your inspection, objects thrown into sharp relief against each other.

Fiction is perhaps closer to film than the stage in this regard, because the writer, like the camera operator has three shots at his or her disposal: the long shot, the medium shot and the close-up. If I can extend Ford Madox Ford's metaphor, imagine you have a state-of-the-art camera with the ability to zoom macro or micro so that whatever is happening on the stage you can film, in whatever detail you choose, from whatever angle you choose. And all it costs is the price of a pen and paper. Writers early in their apprenticeship have a tendency to use mostly long, or mid-range lenses: we get the layout or rooms, and where people are positioned, but nothing on a more intimate scale. And the unfortunate reader has to watch the play from the cheap seats, with no opera glasses.

Make a scene of it

Look for the drama and interest in every scene. If there isn't any, find some. Occasionally scenes are needed for expository purposes to fill the reader in with information. See if you can leaven such a scene with some drama – 'a thing done'. I am reminded of a scene in the Paul Hogan film *Crocodile Dundee II* which could have been dull had they not made a drama out of it: a detective visits our hero while he is having breakfast. Dundee is making toast, and offers the detective some, but then accidentally drops a piece on the floor. Dundee hesitates, and we think he will throw it away, but the man hasn't noticed, so Dundee brushes it off and then puts it on the detective's plate. The necessary but dull information the detective has come to deliver is thus made fascinating as we watch him talking while abstractedly picking pieces of grit from his mouth with every bite of toast he takes. We can do the same on the page if we have imagination and talent.

Setting the emotional scene

The scene you are setting of course, is not purely physical, it is also emotional. So, as well as showing us the fraying counterpane and the cobweb catching the sun, show us human reactions within this setting. Human *reactions*, not concepts. Again, 'showing not telling' is what works best. Imagine you are the film director this time, not the camera operator: how would you show 'lonely', 'depressed', 'happy'? You can't have your characters walking round with signs around their necks. You have to imagine your characters and ask yourself what exactly 'lonely' looks like on their face and in their body.

Particularly with emotional scenes (and don't forget excitement is an emotion) it pays to zoom your reader in close. And I mean *close*. Pupils dilating, hair bristling, palms sweating, chewing on a bottom lip, an eyelid twitching, lips parting, a raised eyebrow: tiny things which can say a lot.

However, don't over-do it. It is sometimes difficult to restrain our enthusiasm for what we are writing, and the purple ink begins to flow. Particularly when dealing with highly emotional scenes, it is worth being restrained. The reader's imagination, if primed properly, can have a hair trigger – one or two clues, and away it goes. Beware a well-intentioned but heavy-handed approach where the reader feels bludgeoned. Again, trust the power of images to evoke. Allow the readers to reach their own conclusions.

Things to try

1 Look around yourself. What objects would you call 'quick', and what 'dead'?
2 If you were a film director, which three details in your present environment would you focus on? What focal length would you use?
3 Take a familiar setting – a room or a landscape – and describe it through unfamiliar eyes.

09

style

In this chapter you will learn:
- to find your own style
- about Fowler's preferences
- what to beware of – use of adjectives, adverbs and abstract nouns, qualifiers, imagery clichés and sentimentality
- to take chances. Be a little daring and bold – willing to fail on the way to your piece of truly inspired writing.

Style is a subject about which many experienced writers have expressed an opinion. And although voiced in different ways, they all say more or less the same thing: style is not something added to a piece of work, it *is* the work. I'm reminded of the story that the poet Benjamin Zephaniah tells of the moment in his boyhood when he became a vegetarian. His mother had served up beefburgers for tea, and – inquiring mind that he had – he asked where beefburgers came from.

> 'They come from cows,' his mother answered.
> 'And where does the cow get them from?' he asked.
> You can imagine his mother's expression when she had to tell him: 'They are the cow.'

Style is the expression of the writer, in the way a beefburger is an expression of the cow. Writing style is not something magicked out of nowhere, unconnected to the author; it is, as Strunk and White say, 'nondetachable'.

> Style is life! It is the very life blood of thought!
>
> *Gustave Flaubert*

Find your own style

The challenge facing us as writers is in finding the perfect expression of who we are, to somehow find ourselves – what we have to say and the voice to say it – so that others can understand perfectly. How to find ourselves? *Not* by wandering round in circles. If we think we know what a writer is, if we keep our heads down and dismiss the idea of a journey of discovery, our writing will never be more than mediocre. We will have found our rut and we will follow it till kingdom come.

If we want to reach for the stars, however, we have to find ourselves. If we want to find ourselves, we have to get lost – to give up all ideas of who we are, who we think we are, who we want to be, who we think we should be. Being a writer is an insecure vocation, not solely for financial reasons, but because writers have to rediscover themselves every day: who am I this morning? What do I believe now? If I open my mouth, what sounds will come out?

Particularly for those of us who are admiring readers, style can be a problem. If it is a quality we enjoy in others, we may long to be able to reproduce such enjoyment. Admiration, however well intentioned, can easily turn to emulation: another rut, but somebody else's in this case.

However, there is value in studying the techniques of others, just as students of painting copy the works of masters. And so, at least at first, I recommend you try out as many different writing styles as you can. Wilfully getting lost, you may discover your own style in the process. Remember, though, that copying is an *exercise*, and the point of an exercise is not to produce an end product, but to furnish us with the skills so that we can write our own story in our own way.

So, beware of adopting another's style as your own: there is a difference between being influenced and copying – one openly acknowledges the provenance, the other is fraudulent. Not only that, but if we adopt another's style wholesale, our writing is likely to be highly self-conscious, perhaps narcissistic. Our eye, as it were, will be on the pen in our hand rather than on our reader's face. And how will perceptive readers react to the fraud? Their instinct will tell them that something is amiss, that the author is walking in someone else's shoes.

> No writing which is self-consciously literature means much to me or means much to the reader – I think he dozes off. But if it sounds right, if it's like a voice in your ear, if it has all the rhythms and surprises of the spoken voice, you are suddenly listening to a living experience – then you know you're getting somewhere.
>
> *Laurie Lee*

Don't try too hard

How to get this naturalness of tone? Simple: stop trying so hard and use language which comes naturally to you. To an outsider this might seem the easiest thing in the world to do, but not so – we don't always know when we're trying too hard. So, watch out for the signs: if you're chewing on your pencil and using your thesaurus for every other word, the chances are you're struggling to be a writer. If you rewrite the same sentence five times, if you find yourself groping for the impressive word, stop it. Forcing yourself to produce a sound which may be against your natural inclination rarely results in anything but cacophony. Your sentences will be leaden and uninspired. The reader will sense the strain, and will be uncomfortable. You will tire easily and wonder why. No fun.

Fowler's preferences

Although there are no rules for good writing style, there are what the Fowler brothers call 'preferences': principles from which to start and only stray from with good reason. They list five in *The King's English*:

Prefer the familiar word to the far fetched

Don't say 'digitigrade' when you mean 'tiptoe'. If your intention is to communicate, use words the average reader should understand without recourse to a dictionary. We may love the sound of particular words, we may love to show off our own erudition; you must remember that this love may not be shared. Usually the only person impressed by our learning is ourselves.

Prefer the single word to the circumlocution

'Circumlocution' means speaking in a roundabout way: valuable in dialogue if it contributes to characterisation, but tedious in non-dialogue. Accuracy and concision are valuable skills to have if you want to hold the reader's attention. Sloppy writing may indicate sloppy thinking, and perceptive readers may consider they are wasting their time.

> The writer does the most, who gives his reader the most knowledge, and takes from his the least time.
>
> *C. C. Colton*

Tautology is a close cousin of circumlocution: this is saying the same thing, in effect, twice. Writing 'He crossed *to the other side of* the road' may not be a heinous crime, but enough of these and the text will have an ill-defined bagginess. Brevity has a lot to do with good style. Like a suit that has been badly cut, extra material can ruin the way a sentence hangs.

Prefer the Saxon to the Romance

Saxon words are those which most commonly feature in colloquial speech. Romance words are those whose roots are Latin. Many writers, under the illusion that literary language equals formal language, write in a way they would rarely speak (with the exception of policemen who 'proceed' instead of 'walk', 'observe' instead of 'see', 'caution' instead of 'warn'). Modern readers are far more informal than their Victorian ancestors: talk to them as you would to friends.

Prefer the short word to the long

That is, unless a long word is better.

I know of only one rule: style cannot be too clear, too simple.

Stendhal

Prefer the concrete to the abstract

This is the most important of the five preferences. Physical senses, because they are all more or less shared by people, are less of a problem than concepts, which by definition are abstract.

Things to beware of

The three 'A's; adjectives, adverbs and abstract nouns

Thinking of a way *not* to begin a novel, the following comes to mind: 'It was a dark and stormy night. He walked slowly to the window and watched the devastation caused by the wind.'

Why do I object to this? (Apart from the opening sentence being famously bad.) The passage more or less sticks to Fowlers' recommendations: the language is everyday, it is concise – little wrong there. But how evocative are the words? How would it have been instead if I wrote: 'The moon was full. He shuffled to the window and watched the storm tearing at the limbs of the willow.' Any more of a picture?

Let's look at these two versions in detail: 'It was a dark and stormy night'. 'Dark' and 'stormy' are *adjectives*, words that describe a noun – 'night' in this case. Adjectives look as though they are doing something important, but are they? Exactly what did I mean by 'dark', and how stormy is 'stormy'? They are clues, to be sure, but they are inexact. A full moon, on the other hand, is exact: we know the quality of light, can picture it for ourselves. 'The storm tearing at the limbs of the willow' is likewise more in focus than 'stormy' alone.

Adjectives, in effect, are a shorthand. 'A beautiful young woman', for instance really means 'You know what I mean. A beautiful young woman is the sort you see in magazines – all cheekbones and doleful eyes.' Multiplying adjectives in the hope of tightening the focus can mean we end up with a list: 'beautiful, almond-shaped, dark eyes' means almost nothing.

An *adverb* is a word which conditions a verb, telling us its quality. There is little justification for writing: 'He walked slowly'. English is a language bursting with verbs – use them. What exactly does the adverb 'slowly' mean? Edge, inch, creep, sidle, dawdle, slide, shuffle, wander, toddle? All these verbs evoke different pictures, and they are all, more or less, slow ways of walking.

Beware unnecessary adjectives: '*happy* sound of laughter', '*gentle* caress' and unnecessary adverbs: 'she whispered *quietly*', 'he stared *fixedly*'. Superfluous adverbs weaken the narrative flow, for instance 'she went to him wordlessly' – if she doesn't say anything it *is* wordless. 'She went to him' is enough. This may seem picky, but anything that is superfluous is dead wood: every word must carry its weight.

Abstract nouns are naming words for states of mind or intellectual concepts or categories. An abstract noun, like an adjective or adverb, means different things to different people: what does 'happiness' mean? Or 'beauty'? 'Devastation', for instance, may mean a few flowerpots blown over, or it may mean an uprooted tree. The second version makes sure there is little misunderstanding: the wind is strong enough to tear at the limbs of the willow – no more, no less. Choosing an image rather than an abstract noun means there is less guesswork needed by your reader.

Qualifiers

Watch our for your use of qualifiers. A qualifier is a word which slightly alters the meaning of another, words such as 'quite', 'often', 'almost'. Qualifiers generally do nothing other than weaken your sentences – cut them out, unless by doing so the meaning of the sentence is significantly altered. What we sacrifice in accuracy, we gain in authority.

> *Rather, very, little, pretty* – these are the leeches that infest the pond of prose, sucking the blood of words ... we should all be very watchful of this rule, for it is a rather important one and we are pretty sure to violate it now and then.
>
> *William Strunk and E B White*

Imagery: metaphor and simile

Abstract nouns are essentially 'telling', rather than 'showing'. Their use assumes readers know what the author intends because they have had a similar experience. But if you think your readers won't have experienced what you are talking about, or need help in imagining it, you can use an image: a metaphor or simile.

'She was overcome by a feeling of complete *isolation*' (abstract noun), would mean different things to different people. 'She felt like a speck on the horizon' (simile), is more evocative, easier to grasp hold of.

Imagery needs to be handled with care: the author can be beguiled into thinking that an ingenious image is an effective one. Imagery may confuse a reader, or draw so much attention to itself that the reader is taken out of the story for a while. Either of these would work against your prime aim: to tell a story. 'Showing' with its no-nonsense literalness usually says more than even a well-chosen image: 'She heard the overpowering silence ringing in her ears', for instance, is probably the best of the three. Beware being poetic just for the sake of it.

> A true poet does not bother to be poetical. Nor does a nursery gardener bother to scent his roses.
>
> *Jean Cocteau*

Clichés, sentimentality, and respecting the reader

A cliché is defined by Fowler as 'a word or phrase whose felicity in a particular context when it was first employed has won it such popularity that it is apt to be used unsuitably or indiscriminately'. The first person who coined the phrase 'as cool as a cucumber' must have been delighted. The second person who said it had coined a cliché. A cliché is second-hand knowledge, betraying a lack of effort by the writer. A writer serving up clichés is in effect feeding his readers warmed-up left-overs.

At what point does sentiment topple over into sentimentality? When the writer is either so self-absorbed he or she has forgotten the readers exist, or when the writer stops respecting their discriminative faculties. Sentimentality is false emotion, failing to recognize, as it does, the complexity of a situation. It is also manipulative of the reader's emotions.

> No one can write decently who is distrustful of the reader's intelligence, or whose attitude is patronizing.
>
> *William Strunk and E. B. White*

Taking chances

I am convinced that writing prose should not be any different from writing poetry. In both cases it is a question of looking for the unique expression, one that is concise, concentrated, and memorable. But digressions and loitering are also valuable.

Italo Calvino

The more we think about style, the more self-conscious we can become, and we find our wings clipped. If we are too concise, too exact, too dutiful in our excision of superfluity, we can find ourselves editing the life out of our work. Digressions and loitering *are* valuable at times. It is worth keeping a certain craziness and irreverence in our writing. Marc Chagall, the Russian expressionist painter, said: 'I like to draw rather badly.' Letting the pen slip in your hand can have a beneficial effect – try it at times. Your job, remember, is to be an artist. There are no points for neatness.

> The whole secret of a living style and the difference between it and a dead style, lies in not having too much style – being in fact a little careless, or rather seeming to be, here and there. It brings wonderful life into the writing.
>
> *Thomas Hardy*

Style is like a person, with all their shortcomings, flashes of brilliance, and vulnerability. A guarded, poised, elegant style may be admired in the way a person with those qualities might, but it will rarely be loved. Readers (with all their shortcomings, flashes of brilliance, vulnerability) want a friend, not a paragon.

Truly inspired writing takes chances. Unless you are willing to fail, you will never fully succeed. Grammar is not a cage within which the writer must live, but a convention formed by usage and improved upon by pedants. Split your infinitives if you like, use a preposition to end a sentence with. Good taste is something to be flouted. If you have a developed ear for language, the chances are you will get away with it.

> Fear of [vulgarity] can be vulgar as anything. Just as a wing three-quarter who's to score in rugby football must generally hug the touch-line, so creative literature, which by its nature involves personal feelings, must run the risk of sentimentality. But it's better to be sometimes sentimental, over-clouded, hyperbolical or merely obvious than to play for safety always and get nowhere. Virgil, Shakespeare, Dickens and countless others were thrust into touch in their time.
>
> *Louis MacNeice*

There is only one way I know to marry spontaneity with discipline so that neither suffer: practise. Write again and again, editing your work with fair but firm hand, developing your craft so that your writing appears effortless. And then when people ask you the reason for your overnight success, you can reply: 'Ten years of practice.'

My feeling about technique in art is that it has about the same value as technique in love-making. That is to say, heartfelt ineptitude has its appeal as does heartless skill; but what you want is passionate virtuosity.

John Barth

60

Things to try

Critically reading your own work is an important, difficult and risky task. Important because self-consciousness is a necessary part of creating a work of art: if we want to improve we need to know our strengths and our weaknesses. Difficult, because critical distance from our own writing can never be truly achieved. And risky because self-consciousness is the enemy of spontaneity. The next two exercises are cautious moves in the direction of becoming self-critical readers.

1 Take a piece of your own writing – perhaps a full chapter if you have one written – and strike out every adjective, adverb and modifier with a pencil. Now, taking a rubber, allow yourself only those words whose presence you can justify.

2 Read a piece of your own writing over and over – both aloud and silently. Listen to the music of your sentences, ignoring the meaning. Notice any repetitiveness or cacophony. Mark sentences which appear clumsy, and then rewrite them, listening with your inner ear.

Transferring this rigour to the writing process can help you get it right first time. The next exercise is very restrictive, and I don't recommend you hold yourself in such tight restraint as a matter of course.

3 Write a passage in 300 words, using no adverbs, adjectives or abstract nouns, describing one of the following:
   • A novice nun walking the length of a corridor, at the end of which is a thick studded door. Tall windows flood the corridor with light.
   • A person on the flat roof of a tall city building, looking at the bustling city life below.

- An attendant in a Turkish bath soaping the back of a fat and hairy man.

  When the piece is complete, add one adjective.

4 Take a passage from a novel by a writer whose style you admire. Analyze each sentence, looking for the author's use of verbs, nouns, adjectives, adverbs and qualifiers. What is the effect of their technical choices? Now write one of the scenes of exercise 1 in the style of this author. Compare the effect of the original version with the second version.

10

theme

In this chapter you will learn:
- about subject matter and genre
- about thread, the unifying idea through your story
- about thesis, which causes readers to revisit the book, debate and discuss, even after they have finished reading it.

Theme is the heart of a story. Sometimes the theme will be clear before the first word is written, or sometimes the writer will start with a hunch and use the novel to discover exactly what to say. Either is fine; whether the theme is the impulse which gets you going or the point of arrival doesn't matter. What matters is that you have a theme, because without one, a story will never fully satisfy a reader, regardless of how well written it is, or how exciting, or how clever.

So, what is this important thing called 'theme'? The word is used to mean so many different things I would like to drop its use for the duration of this chapter. In its place I suggest three levels of distinction:

- subject matter
- thread
- thesis

Subject matter

The subject matter of the story is its tangible reality. The subject matter of *Jack and the Beanstalk*, for instance, is the consequences of selling a cow for five magic beans. If you hear someone say there are no original stories left to be told, they can't be referring to subject matter, for as the world is infinitely various, so is subject matter.

Genre fiction has a lot to say about subject matter, and if your novel falls into an obvious genre category, you should know what the current trends are. Having a good solid knowledge of similar genre novels is important, likewise knowing what others have said about such books. Trends, however, change quickly so you also need to keep your reading up to date. And not just of fiction: by the time a novel is in the bookshop it contains ideas at least two or three years old. So, read newspapers, appropriate magazines, subscribe to a SF magazine, join the Romantic Novelists' Association. Find out what other people are thinking and talking and writing about.

Try to spot trends – political, social, scientific. Make a friend of Michael Crichton and find out how he always seems to spot a trend before anyone else.

If you want to raise your chances of making money, find a so-called 'high profile' subject and give it an upbeat ending. You may not find a place in the twentieth-century hall of literary fame, but you may find an audience.

The recipe for an Oscar winner: show a protagonist overcoming adversity against a background that exorcises the audience's guilt about an uncomfortable subject.

Steve de Souza

Thread

A high-profile idea may get an editor's attention. Keeping it is another matter. This is where the thread plays its part. I use the word 'thread' for this level of distinction because, like a thread of cotton you might tie from tree to tree in an enchanted forest, it can help you retrace your steps if you get lost. A thread is a unifying idea, a line of thought that leads through a story upon which the plot events are strung like beads. There are a limited number of threads, the most obvious being:

love	survival	guilt
greed	glory	revenge
justice	redemption	power
freedom	self-awareness	vanity

The thread of *Jack and the Beanstalk*? It depends how you tell it, but you could make a good case for 'greed'. Most novels contain a number of threads, in which case they should be plaited, that is intricately combined.

Perhaps the best way to give an example of how threads combine is to tell you a complete story. This is one by the American writer, Leonard Michaels.

The hand

I smacked my little boy. My anger was powerful. Like justice. Then I discovered no feeling in the hand. I said, 'Listen, I want to explain the complexities to you.' I spoke with seriousness and care, particularly of fathers. He asked when I finished, if I wanted him to forgive me. I said yes. He said no. Like trumps.

This is a classic plot – albeit rather brief. Although the story is not intended to stand alone (being a part of a collection of similar tales), it *is* a completed process of change, which upon close examination follows the eight-point arc. (Implied stastis; trigger is smacking the boy; quest to retain self-justification; the surprise is the hand going numb; critical choice to ask for forgiveness; climax, the son refuses to accept the apology; reversal, from dominant to dominated; implied resolution).

The subject matter is always obvious: here, a father hitting his child and the conversation which follows. The threads of this tale are more a matter of personal interpretation: I think guilt and power are the threads in this case.

Thesis

The third level of distinction is that of thesis. This is the most important part of the three levels, the way to hold the editor's attention through the book *and* beyond. Whether readers can identify the thesis for themselves or not, it is what causes rumination after the book is finished, the element which generates debate and disagreement. And of the three levels, it is the most neglected by writers.

What is thesis? It can be defined simply as: *what the author is saying about the thread summed up in a single sentence.*

> The impulse to write a novel comes from a momentary unified vision of life.
>
> *Angus Wilson*

There is a story of how Winston Churchill once waved away a pudding in a restaurant after a single mouthful with the words: 'Take this pudding away. It has no theme.' A discriminating reader may say much the same thing about a novel with no thesis. A unified vision of life doesn't mean it has to be profound, but it can't be too confused. A pudding which is half baked Alaska and half rhubarb crumble is confused. And anyway, most of us aren't seeking profundity from stories any more than we are seeking them from puddings. But we are seeking *comprehensibility*.

Let's look more closely at our definition of thesis.

What the author – in other words, *you*: (not society, not received wisdom, not tradition)

is saying about the thread – what are you saying about greed? (What is Leonard Michaels saying about guilt and power?)

summed up in a single sentence – if the best you can come up with is a long and waffling explanation, it may be a sign your thesis needs attention. It may not be easy to do, you may have to think about it for months (I know I do), you may not know the thesis until you have reached the end of the book. In fact, many books are extended debates between parts of the author. By the end the parts may agree to differ, or they may be integrated, either way they should reach a conclusion.

A narrative is an argument stated in fictional terms.

Angela Carter

Don't let yourself off the hook with this. Being able to pin your thesis down – a kind of mission statement for the novel – will pay off. A clearly-defined thesis can bring an entire novel into focus. A novel may be an argument, but it shouldn't be a stand-up row.

And a thesis, regardless of the complexity of the tale, *can* always be summed up in a single sentence (albeit a long one in some cases) without doing too much damage to its complexity. It was Einstein (I think) who said that anyone who couldn't explain his work to an eight year old is a charlatan.

It is perhaps *thesis* that people mean when they talk about a limited number of stories. But it is not the originality of your thesis, nor even its depth, which counts so much as the way you present it. Some perennial favourites:

crime doesn't pay	you can't keep a good man down
love conquers all	hell hath no fury like a woman winner
takes all	scorned the truth will out

The thesis (and to some extent the thread) is not inherent in the bare bones of the story, its appearance figuring only in the telling. This is where the personality of the writer comes in: a single storyline can be presented in quite different lights without tampering too much with the eight-point arc. If any proof of this were needed, read about the same event in different newspapers. Without even distorting the facts, two very different views of a single event can be presented, depending on the prejudices and beliefs of the journalist.

Not only does the thesis depend on the telling, it depends on the interpretation by the reader. The meaning of a story, therefore, will always be open to debate – a fact for which critics are forever grateful, keeping them, as it does, in work. What is the meaning of the Leonard Michaels story? That guilt which turns to self-righteousness can be turned against the guilty? That the apparently powerless can still win the day? In a way, it is irrelevant if our understanding of the story differs from that of the author; what counts is that the author is clear in his own mind what he is doing. In this way, whether the story is completely successful or not, it will at least have a ring of authority.

Not every novel you read will have a clearly identifiable thesis: this may be because the author didn't manage to convey it in a way you could understand, or wasn't clear in the first place. Such books are often like low-grade fast food: tasty in an obvious sort of way, but without much nutrition. They can also leave you hungry, not because of a shortage of bulk, but because there's no substance behind the fizz and pop. The market for junk food and junk literature is ever-expanding, and there is a lot of money to be made. Whatever sort of writing you are drawn to write, don't resist the tug. If you self-consciously inject meaning into your work, you will probably seem fake. Even junk has its own integrity.

The function of plot is to communicate the thesis. More than anything, stories fall down because of a lack of coherence. A series of events with little significance outside the drama of the story may just scrape by as a plot, but it will rarely outlive its creator.

Know your thesis

If the thread is a trail of cotton tied from tree to tree, the thesis is a compass keeping you pointing in the right way. If you have no compass, you won't know which way to go, and could end up wandering for years. A wandering plot lacks shape because the directionless author doesn't know what fits in the story and what doesn't. Because, just as important as knowing what you *are* writing about is knowing what you are *not* writing about. A story which contains too many threads and not enough thesis is like a stew with too many ingredients – it ends up tasting of everything and nothing.

Plot events should be considered in the light of what you are saying about the thread: if 'crime doesn't pay' is your thesis (the thread could be greed), how would a scene between the criminal and his long-suffering partner contribute to that? It may legitimately contradict it: we may think for a while that crime *does* pay. Fine, as long as it is doing something there.

For every chapter, and every scene, you should ask yourself: what is it doing here? What does it say about the thesis?

> The most important thing in a work of art is that it should have a kind of focus, that is, there should be some place where all the rays meet or from which they issue.
>
> *Leo Tolstoy*

Hopefully your structure will tell your readers what the thesis is without the need for explanation. You know you're on shaky ground when you have your characters doing a lot of talking at the end of the book; your readers may get the idea you're trying to explain your way out of a tight corner. Drama is about *action*, remember. A good plot is the manifestation of an idea in concrete, observable ways. You should be able to mime a good story and still convey the thesis.

The critical choices of your characters should be congruent with the thesis. If you can see no clear link between events precipitated by characters and what the story is saying, then you may find it is a weak link. If you sense a lull in activity in the middle of your book and throw in an exciting scene whose only function is to wake the reader up, then your reader may be confused. What was the meaning of the scene? they'll think. Why did a man with a gun suddenly burst in and then leave for no apparent reason? Such a scene may be one you have slaved over. You may be proud of its every word. It may contain the mostly finely honed sentences of your life. But if it doesn't contribute to the thesis, cut it out. Don't throw it away – you might be able to use it. Or if it's so good, shelve the novel and keep the scene. Whatever, don't be tempted to think that just because it is your favourite scene, your readers will love it. If it doesn't contribute to the thesis, they'll wonder what it is doing there.

Things to try

1 Think of the most recent novel you read, or film you saw. What were its threads? What was its thesis?
2 Analyze your work in progress. What are the threads? Do you have a thesis yet?

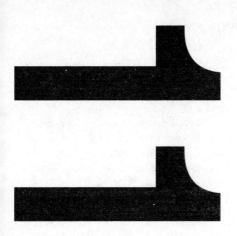

11

editing and shaping

In this chapter you will learn:
- to let yourself write, no holds barred, and to rewrite and edit at a later date
- how to expand on your first draft and shape your novel, thematically and aesthetically
- about the temporal pace of a novel and how to handle the passage of time
- how to finish your book.

Writing and editing

Writing is not a single process. There are two activities at work when we are writing a novel, and we confuse them at our peril. There is the inspirational stage when we pluck ideas out of the ether, and there is the craft stage when we order this vision so that it makes sense. The first I call writing, the second I call editing. It is important to keep the two separate, not trying to write and edit at the same time. If you are the sort of person who is correcting the beginning of a sentence before you reach the end, you are trying to do contradictory things at the same time, that is, be imaginative and be ordered. Writing and editing at the same time is like trying to run a race while tying your shoe laces: some forwards movement perhaps, but no chance of winning the race.

This confusion of domains is the single biggest obstacle to most beginners. Although editing is essential in creating a coherent work of art, it is of secondary importance to inspiration. After all, you can only edit something which is on the page. If your internal editor gets out of hand, you may have nothing on the page except a hundred crossings out.

My advice? Let yourself write what you want to write – no holds barred. When the ink has dried, *then* see whether it makes sense. A tip to help keep the two separate: try writing an entire first draft without reading back once (I did this with my second novel with the result that I wrote the first draft in six weeks). If this is too much, reduce the scale. Finish a whole chapter without reading back, or if *that's* too much, an entire scene. Breaking the flow of inspiration is never a good idea; sometimes it can have disastrous consequences for your writing. Like groping after an ill-remembered dream, we can feel the details of the story slipping through our fingers.

> In all the arts the great problem of the artist is to preserve the force of his intuition, his germ, what is sometimes called his inspiration, throughout the long process of technical construction.
>
> *Joyce Cary*

Rewriting is essential. Sometimes the words will come out right the first time, in which case leave well alone. As in life, so in fiction: if it ain't broke, don't fix it. Having your words come out right first time will probably happen more often the more experience you have. However, even master storytellers can benefit from a cool-headed appraisal of the original vision.

But don't over-edit. Sometimes, in our anxiety to produce our best, we can refine all the charm and character out of our work. A certain roughness can have an appeal, and the crazy chinks between reason are often those gaps through which our reader's imagination can escape.

Too much polishing weakens rather than improves a work.

Pliny the Younger

Editing sentences and paragraphs is a matter of getting a feel for the music of the language, checking your coherence – the tenses, your viewpoint, that it's working as a piece of language. Brevity counts for a lot. Be bold: superfluity, whether of individual words or paragraphs, scenes or even chapters, will not help you achieve greatness. Better a slim book which leaves the reader wanting more than a fat one which is hard to get through.

When in doubt, cut.

Ford Madox Ford

Shaping the novel

The most important shaping factor in the plot, as I said in Chapter 10, is the *thesis*. The essence of the novel is what you're saying about the subject. If you don't know what you're saying, the structure will reflect that and you will have a lopsided story or a story with bits falling off it. In other words, it will probably lack a satisfying shape.

Understanding your thesis will give you a thematic shape, but it won't necessarily give you an aesthetic shape, and you need both for a successful novel. You don't just want a novel which makes sense, you want a novel which has an aesthetic coherence. Although there are no rules for shaping a classic plot, few would argue with Aristotle's insistence upon a beginning, middle and end. We may have heard this many times without fully understanding it; using the language of the eight-point arc, we can say:

> beginning = stasis, trigger and quest
> middle = surprises, critical choices and climax
> end = reversal and resolution.

The comedy writer Danny Simon puts it simpler still: the beginning is the 'want', the middle is the 'conflict', and the end is the 'resolution'.

Having successfully assured yourself that your novel features all three parts, how can you approach an overall aesthetic structure? I like to think of a narrative ski slope, except the reader is travelling in reverse:

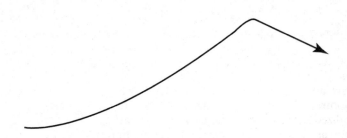

Tension should mount throughout the story, reaching a satisfying climax close to the end. Although there is pleasure to be gained from the 'dying fall', a quiet period after the climax, beware of making it too long, otherwise we will have anticlimax. Also watch our for making the rising tension relentless. Unless your readers have time to catch their breath, they will feel battered by the end. So, pace your story with andante passages, lulls in the action:

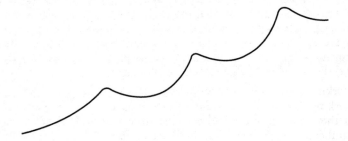

Something that I do in desperation when I'm editing my novels is to use another medium to get a sense of shape, such as the line drawing above. I use anything I can think of: a song, or a piece of music, or drawing coloured patterns, or pie charts, or bar graphs – anything which will help me get a feel for the shape of the novel. Stranger things have been done in the name of story writing.

Because there are no rules, you have to feel your way into this. Basically what you're going for is some part of the brain that can 'get' it in one. Paintings you can get in one, poems – if they're short enough – you can get in one; films because of their temporal aspect you can do likewise. Music is perhaps the best because it is the most uncerebral of the lot.

With my fourth novel, I was searching for the tone of it, the feel of it. My plotting was done, but there was something missing. I had the graph, as it were, but not the colour. Then I heard a song, one I knew previously, and I listened to the lyrics, and I realized how appropriate they were to what I was saying. The words captured the emotional flavour of the novel perfectly, and I realized the 'colour' of the novel I was searching for: *pathos*. As soon as I knew that, I realized what could fit in and what couldn't – for instance, a certain type of crass humour would have to go, nor could I have my protagonist be too self-pitying.

Play with paints, building blocks, clay. See if you can sculpt your novel to find this aesthetic coherence which is so important.

Working chronologically

Some writers (myself included) start at the beginning of the story and work chronologically, and some write a patchwork of scenes, stitching them together at the end. Choose whichever method suits you best; however, realize that you have to imagine yourself as a reader approaching the story for the first time, not an easy task even when you are approaching from the same direction. Disrupting the order of telling and assembling them at the end may mean you have trouble grasping the story's tempo, and the emotional development of the narrative.

Working chronologically requires writers to defer gratification, working through the dull-but-necessary parts before they get on to the excitement. Sometimes this may feel like painting by numbers, but patience has its own prize: the heightening of anticipation as you near a dramatic scene is one of the main pleasures of writing, a pleasure which hopefully is reflected in the telling.

Whether you work chronologically or not is not important: what counts is a seamless finished product. The reader's eye should not be drawn to the construction of the story (that is, unless you intend ironic or unsettling effects). You want the reader to be engrossed in a story which has all the inevitability of gravity.

Excision and expansion

Editing involves both excision and expansion. Excision means cutting off any fat from the bone, retracing your steps from any wrong turnings you have taken. Part of the writing of a novel is exploratory – you're not going to know the entire map before you start, so inevitably there will be scenes that don't belong, or are out of place.

Real literature, like travel, is always a surprise.

Alison Lurie

In my first book, I cut out about a third of the initial draft, representing a year's work. If this needs to be done, there is nothing else for it: be strong, be brave; the quality of the finished work is everything.

Now, my editing is almost always a matter of expansion, particularly of my characters. When I revisit a scene on the rewrite, my understanding is invariably deeper: not only of the characters, but of their place in the action. At the end of the book, when I look back at chapter one, I spot the necessary changes to the plot.

The rewrite is probably the place you will develop sub-plot. On the first trawl through the book, your attention will mainly be on the main plot, just getting to the end of the book without it all falling apart. When you do reach the end of the first draft, heave a sigh of relief, congratulate yourself, and then start again, filling in the non-essential parts of the story.

Pace

A novel has a temporal aspect, even though strictly speaking it doesn't dictate its duration, as a film does. Although you can read a book over five years or five days, the pace of a story is important. You may not be aware of it when you're writing: when you're right in the moment of creativity, you probably won't be aware of the passage of narrative time. It is only on reflection that you will see whether a scene is too fast or too slow. Too fast and you'll leave your readers unsatisfied, reading the same scene twice in the hope of prolonging their pleasure. Too slow and the story will drag, and they will be bored and start skipping pages.

What if it *is* too fast? How can you slow the action so that your scene has the maximum dramatic impact, without bogging it down with unnecessary detail? I can think of four ways I have used: focussing on small detail, using slow-motion (as it were); using interiors, that is, stopping time; using the *ritardando* effect of adjectives and adverbs; adding dialogue.

For instance:

> She drew back her hand and slapped his cheek

could become:

> She drew back her hand, her perfectly manicured fingernails like claws. This is going to hurt her more than it hurts me, he thought, as she slapped his cheek hard. 'Ow!' he yelped. He rubbed his stinging face. I was wrong, he thought ruefully.

Speeding up a scene is easier: you do the reverse. Cut out anything – dialogue too – which doesn't contribute to the action. And so we're back to 'She drew back her hand and slapped his cheek', or just 'She slapped his cheek'.

What if the plot itself is progressing too quickly? This is where you can develop the subplot. Or try introducing a new character. Also check your levels of conflict (see Chapter 2) and if one level is missing introduce a new source of antagonism. But whatever you do, don't waffle, don't pad it out just for the sake of it. You may have written a beautiful story which happens to be on the slim side: Sagan's *Bonjour Tristesse*, Camus' *The Outsider*, Hesse's *Siddhartha* – there is no shortage of lean books which could have been spoiled by an anxious fattening-up process.

Handling the passage of time

A recurrent problem for apprentice novelists is the handling of the passage of time. If our action happens on day 1, 2 and 4, what do we do with the problematic day 3? Do we dutifully fill in the detail, hoping the reader won't notice that nothing of importance is happening? No. As with choosing any detail, selection is the key: some events are so important that we want to slow the pace right down; some events are irrelevant, in which case they should be excised. Your reader is not interested in events for their own sake (this is E. M. Forster's 'story'), but in their relevance to each other (in other words, plot.) If an event has no bearing on plot, do everyone a favour – leave it out.

Drama is like real life with the dull bits cut out.

Alfred Hitchcock

What are the technicalities of cutting the dull bits out? The solution most writers use is simplicity itself. If the time gap is between chapters, begin the fresh chapter 'Two days later', or 'The next summer'. If there are just one or two gaps of time within a chapter, it is probably best to leave a double space to indicate the passage of time. Otherwise a fresh paragraph would do.

Most readers are probably more sophisticated than we give them credit for, in which case they will probably work out the time gap for themselves without the helping hand of 'Two days later'. A double space alone will often be enough to tell them time has passed – they can guess how much if they need to.

Is it a problem if the action of Chapter 1 happens entirely on a spring day, and Chapter 2 is spread over a month? I don't think so: most readers are accustomed to the erratic progression of time. They will assume that nothing of importance happened in the hiatus, and so accept that the story is progressing in this way. However, there is probably something to be said for symmetry and regularity: I might have a problem with a very long time gap in an otherwise compact novel. E. M. Forster took a chance with *A Passage to India*, introducing a gap of two years in an otherwise compact time scheme, a gap not entirely satisfactorily bridged by dividing the book into three parts.

The flashback

A flashback is the introduction of a scene of an earlier event into a current situation, probably more often used in cinema than in fiction. There is no inherent difficulty in writing flashback: it is a normal scene in every way apart from its placement. If you meet any problem in using it, it will be in the join between past and present. Again, it is worth respecting the reader's intelligence; unless the time of the scene needs to be identified, it isn't necessary to head the scene with a date. A fresh chapter, or a double space is enough of an indicator, and if you want to rapidly orientate your reader, give a clue or two in the first line that we have gone back in time.

Although there are no rules to any of this, there is something you should keep in mind: any disruption of time and space in the novel should be justifiable. If the display of technical virtuosity is to be something more than spectacle, it has to contribute in an important way to the telling of the tale.

The 'back story'

If you find yourself needing to inform the reader of something that happened in the past, and are reluctant to disrupt the chronology with flashback, there are several options. Here are four ways I filled in the 'back story' in my novel, *The Life Game*. The characters are those of a thirtysomething English woman and a man who is giving her shelter for the night in his cottage.

Speech

> 'So, tell me something about yourself,' he said with his mouth full. 'You're not from these shores, I can tell that.'
> 'No, I'm from England – London. I came here on holiday.'

Speech is the most obvious method. Talking to each other is the way we mostly get to know each other's pasts, though beware making it sound too expository. I chose dialogue in the above example, because – although the reader doesn't know it yet – she is lying to him.

Thoughts (monologue) or reverie

I find myself most often using character's thoughts to fill in the reader. It is more personal and honest (unless we have an unreliable narrator), and allows you to convey the sort of information characters might want to keep to themselves.

> It came to her: an image of watching him paint, one Saturday, lying on the bed, a stripe of shadow from the window moving across the floor as the afternoon slipped by, drowsing in the heat and smoke and the sleepy sound of traffic.
>
> She stooped to pick up the spade, and started work again.

Summary

> She went up to her room to get her diary. She'd kept a diary since the age of sixteen. Paul had thought she was neurotic about it, but it was her touchstone, the most constant companion she'd had throughout her life.

Summary of this type is perhaps the most straightforward way of giving information about the past. It has the advantage of concision, but because it is passive, too much of it will dull the telling of your tale.

Diaries, letters, press cuttings

> **June 1st**
> I think I'm in lust. I met Paul again today. It surprised me – I'd given up on him after a week had gone by without hearing from him, but he phoned me and invited me to his studio-cum-flat on the Hammersmith Road.

This last device – the equivalent of a character coming onto stage to report off-stage calamities in Greek theatre – is the most barefaced of all the options. This is perhaps as hackneyed as portraying the passage of time in film by showing a calendar whose leaves are being torn off, but although you won't get marks for originality, it is a technique still worth considering.

Gaining perspective

The challenge of editing is putting yourself in the mind of an imaginary person who is reading it for the first time. Jane Austen used to put a manuscript away in a drawer for a year before she read it again and edited it. If you have the time and patience for this, try it by all means. The further back from the work you can get, the better a sense of perspective you will have. I'm reminded of watching cinema hoarding artists in India: I used to love watching them paint these huge pictures flat on the ground before them – matinee idols as big as houses, faces the size of cars, teeth like hubcaps – and then hoist them above the cinema. By some miracle, everything would be in proportion. But don't assume that because one person can do it, you can do it too: give yourself as much time and space as you can. Take a long walk back from your novel, squint your eyes and look at it as if you've never seen it before. Only then will you see if the eyes are crossed and the nose is where the ear should be.

Getting feedback

This is where asking for other people's feedback is so useful: they won't have seen the picture before. So, when to show your work? Not too early. Keep your own counsel, at least at first. This is *your* book, *your* vision of the world. Premature exposure could confuse you if you get conflicting opinions, bedazzle you if the feedback is flattering, or crush you if it is damning.

And be careful who you show it to: showing a novel to the wrong person can have a disastrous effect on writers who are unsure of themselves. When I am working on a book (including this one), I already have in mind the people who I want to read it for me. Close friends and family are not always the best critics of your work: they know you too well, and they may hold fire if they think it will hurt your feelings. I choose people for specific reasons: someone to check my technical accuracy, or psychological insight, or theory.

When you get their feedback, listen carefully but also realize that one person's opinion is just that. There is no final judge, regardless of status. If you need reminding of this, just read different reviews of the same novel. And so try it out on three or four people, enough to get a balance of feedback and see if there is any consensus of opinion.

Novel length and chapter length

How long should a novel be? About the length of a piece of string, perhaps a little longer. A novel has no set lengths, obviously. A novel is a cultural convention, it doesn't have to obey any laws of physics. But in terms of marketing, anything less than 60,000 words will make a publisher anxious – they will have to use large type. Anything less than 40,000 words and it's a novella, smaller still and it's a short story. Unless you're very well known, or a genius, most editors would back off from very short novels: it may be a very good book, but the marketing department has to think in terms of value for money. The average novel is about 80,000 to 120,000 words. Doorstoppers weigh in at around 200,000 words. Unless you're working in genre fiction, there is no set length within these extremes. Beware of trying to fit your story into a certain shape or length. Certainly in the first draft, I recommend you think only of what is coming next, not how long it will pan out. I have found that working this way, all my novels have come out at more or less standard sizes.

What about chapter length? Likewise you can have very short chapters, or very long chapters, or indeed no chapters at all. The average number of chapters per novel is between 20 and 40. The number isn't important: the main thing is regularity. If you have one chapter of 3,000 words and the next one of 6,000 words, that might cause a problem for the readers (who after all, are the final arbiters of your novelistic decisions – at least while they're reading the book). Readers are becoming increasingly tolerant of diversions from the norm, as the novel is being stretched in very different shapes. Break the convention by all means. The only question to ask is: does it work?

Finishing your book

At what point can you say that your novel is finished? *Not* when you have come to the end of the first draft, though I once met a published author who only ever wrote single drafts of her novels. At the time I was too stunned to ask her how she managed this, and so I am still trying to figure it out. How could there not be room for improvement? Looking at my first drafts, there are *mansions* of room for improvement.

The first draft of a novel is usually a thinking aloud, an exploratory piece full of gaps and superfluities. This is no bad thing: holding the pen loosely in the hand *will* result in mistakes, but it will also encourage the author to take chances, some of which will pay off. If you think you have to get it right first time, you may succeed in having an unblotted copy book, but the quality of the writing may be nothing more than mediocre, the plot nothing more than pedestrian. Take chances with your first version: it is the job of the second, third, fourth drafts to deal with the chances that failed, cutting them out or changing them into a workable plot.

When my first draft is complete, I ask for other people's feedback. This takes some courage, for the manuscript is far from presentable at this stage, but any sooner and I may be in danger of writing *their* book, any later and I may be loath to make any necessary changes. And the changes that are needed after the initial draft are likely to be substantial – we're not talking about decorating yet, this is a matter of architecture. Getting feedback too late may put you in a difficult position. It is hard enough to tear a narrative wall down when it is unplastered, but when it has been painted and papered, it is almost impossible.

Sometimes, of course, great works come out in one – and I think here of Mozart. But for every person like this there are a hundred scribblers and scratchers. Look at an original score of Beethoven's to see that works of genius don't always come out clean.

An image I've heard used to describe the redrafting of a book is that of lacing up a tall boot. You start at the toe and then loosely lace up to the top. Then you return to the toe and tighten up to the top again, making minor adjustments. So, how many tightenings is enough? Every writer is different: I usually do four drafts, the final one involving subtle changes to characterization and syntax.

It is at this stage someone has to take it from my hands and send it to my publishers, for I have a very real reluctance to let go of it.

> The book dies a real death for me when I write the last word. I have a little sorrow and then I go on to a new book which is alive.
>
> *John Steinbeck*

The sweet-sour feeling of placing the final full stop on the page is, for me, always tempered with hesitancy. Is it really finished? Perhaps one more tightening is needed? As this point I remind myself of the story of the never-ending novel. It goes like this:

there was once a novelist who wrote a very long book. It took him ten years of hard work. When he reached the end and read back what he had written, he realized that he was no longer the person of ten years ago. His wisdom had deepened, his skill had increased. And so he sat down to rewrite the book. Ten more years passed. When he reached the end of this second draft, he read back what he had written. Again, he realized that he was no longer the person who had begun the rewrite. His wisdom was deeper still, his skill more profound. And so he sat down to rewrite it a third time ...

It was Apollinaire, I think, who said that you don't finish a poem so much as abandon it. The same is true of a novel. There is no point of arrival, no point of perfection. You just do your best with what you've got, cross your fingers and send your creation out into the world. *Then* you get on with the next project, resolving – if you are like me – not to make the same mistakes as last time.

Things to try

1 Make forward progress by not editing and writing at the same time. If you can, don't even read what you've written until you reach the end of the story.
2 Draw a graph, using different coloured pens to chart the progress of:
   (a) different characters
   (b) main plot and subplot.
3 Ask yourself these questions: How may acts (that is, major reversals) does the plot divide into? Does each act climax top the previous one?

12

the personality
of the writer

In this chapter you will learn:
- about what makes someone
  an artist
- about how a writer
  experiences the world
- the importance of putting
  yourself in the shoes of your
  reader.

Until now we have been talking about the craft of novel writing. Now we venture into the misty landscape of what it means to be an artist. You may dismiss the notion of being a writer-as-artist for any number of reasons: I just want to tell stories, you may say. I know nothing about art. I don't have what it takes to be an artist. But you are already an artist: anybody who has any aesthetic sense at all is an artist. Anybody who sees value in non-utilitarian activity is an artist. Anybody who wants to tell stories is an artist.

The problems surrounding the word 'artist' are similar to those surrounding the word 'writer'. These words are groaning under the weight of significance, none of them of any help to us. We need to talk about it though, for under the denial, or embarrassment, or pride is something that needs to be claimed if we are to hit our stride as a writer of novels. Only when we claim our artistic nature can we develop it: everyone may be an artist, but some are clearly better than others. Why? Part of it is innate talent, and part of it is the courage to develop something within us that may expose our vulnerability.

> Everyone has talent. What is rare is the courage to follow
> that talent to the dark place where it leads.
>
> *Erica Jong*

The sensibility of the artist

There are many myths surrounding the notion of the talented artist. One of them is that the artist has a high degree of skill, an ability with words or paint or movement that is out of the ordinary. This may be true in part; however, it is not a defining characteristic. What makes a person an artist is not what they have, but what they do with what they have. (Similarly with a genius. IQ tests of people regarded as geniuses indicate their average to be 120. High, to be sure, but hardly freakish: what makes them special is the degree of creativity they exhibit with their intelligence.)

Being an artist has very little to do with skill. Being an artist is a matter of sensibility, that is, how you relate to the world – the *real world* of tea cups and sunsets and falling leaves and other human beings. This relationship is open to us all, regardless of our talent. If you want to develop as a writer, it is this relationship which you must first develop.

The genius keeps all his days the vividness and intensity of interest that a sensitive child feels in this expanding world.
Dorothea Brande

What characterizes an 'artistic' relationship? If we look at some definitions of creativity we may come close to an answer. Nicola de Carlo in *Psychological Games* defines creativity as: 'The capacity to see new relationships, to entertain out-of-the-ordinary ideas and to free our intuition from traditional ways of thinking.' Lucia Cappachione defines it as: 'The ability to break through to new understanding or expression beyond what one has experienced before.' Both are saying more or less the same thing, although they use only one word in common: new. The artist is a person who relates to the world in a new way.

Caring about the world

Hand in hand with this sensibility go two qualities, the first of which is caring about the world in which you live. There is one thing all artists share: an inordinate interest in the world. Most writers are the sort of people to dismantle a perfectly good clock just to see how it works. Writers – all artists, I think – are people who are fascinated by the world and its inhabitants. Some of them are delighted, as William Blake was, or appalled, as Franz Kafka was, but they are all inquisitive, searching. The writerly personality is one which wishes to open other people's mail; or cries at news bulletins; or wishes they could spend all day finishing sentences which begin 'What if..?'; or ignores the headlines and goes straight to the two-inch item at the bottom of the page which reads: 'Boy saves fish from drowning'. You need to care for the subject matter of your writing – that is, people and things and the extraordinariness of it all. If you despise your characters, or your subject matter, or your readers, your book will repel people.

The passion for self-expression

The second quality the writer needs is a passion for putting things down on paper. Why? The reasons are irrelevant: all that counts is the compulsion to make your mark, to say 'I was here. My life mattered', whether it is handprints on Neolithic cave walls or smuggled poetry written on concentration camp paper.

We have lived; our moments are important. This is what it is to be a writer: to be the carriers of details that make up history.
Natalie Goldberg

Depth of personality

There are two stages in developing this relationship of 'newness' between the writer and the world: what I have called perception and selection. Developing your perception means seeing things which other people might miss – and seeing not just with your eyes, but with your whole body.

The ability to select comes next: taking what is important and leaving what is not. Selection is where your aesthetic judgement comes into play, a matter of depth of personality rather than skill alone. We are in very misty territory indeed now, and there are no answers to the questions this raises. What is depth of personality? Can we deepen ourselves? Are some of us doomed to be perpetually shallow? To express a personal view, one I feel is right but can't prove, I would say that there are no limits to the depth of our personality – with no exceptions. We all have extraordinary abilities and insight and understanding, we all have infinitely complex thought patterns and emotional responses. Some of us may not be willing to climb into the bathysphere and explore our emotional depths. Fine – why should we? But we are all able to, if we wish.

If you *do* wish, it is important to know that without these two abilities – perception and selection – all the other qualities you admire in others and wish for yourself, such as wisdom, profound insight, wit, intelligence, will remain elusive.

The anatomy of the writer

The body may seem an unlikely topic in a discussion about writers, but your body is the foundation of your experience. Who you perceive yourself to be is very much – for all but the angels among us – grounded in a physical reality. You are incarnate, and so are your readers. Writers experience the world not as abstract ideas, but physically: snagging a sleeve on a splinter; the smell of coffee and diesel fumes; a lover brushing the nape of the neck – real events which make up our day. These things are the basis of reality. Everything else, theories, opinions and conclusions, is made up.

It may be tempting to think of art, particularly a non-tangible art such as writing, as very abstract, as very pure and unmuddied with physicality. You may say the reason you write is to break the bonds of your physicality with the magic of imagination and language, that the point of reading is to leave behind the limitations of the everyday world. And I would agree: this is certainly the reason I write. When I'm writing, I am at my most free; and yes, I want to free my readers. But freedom is a concept, and concepts exist in only one place: the mind. The most effective way of getting to the mind, I believe, is by passing through the gates of the body. In other words 'show, don't tell'.

It's worth taking a closer look at the anatomy of a writer. What aspects of ourselves do we need to develop so we can become more of an artist?

Eyes and ears

These help us to see the unique in the everyday. Have you watched babies boggling at the world, considered the extraordinariness of a tree, the preposterous improbability of a cat? If we could learn to be more childlike and less adult, we might find our words springing off the page. Mediocrity, mechanicalness, utilitarianism, the oh-I-know-the-world-it's-like-this-ness are deadening influences. The artistic impulse is organic, chaotic, fresh. It's about breaking free of the deadening influence of routine so that something new can be brought into existence.

What we need is not brilliant insights or sophisticated reasoning so much as simplicity and naivety. The *Emperor's New Clothes* is a salutary tale for us all. We need to view the world as if we are new-born at every moment.

> Little minds are interested in the extraordinary; great minds in the commonplace.
>
> *Elbert Hubbard*

The writer of genius sees the unique in the everyday, the extraordinary in the ordinary. This is not a matter of huge dramas: it is a matter of seeing the huge drama in the apparently prosaic, a matter of waking up to the power and extraordinary nature of the world in which we live.

Don't forget your nose, your skin, your taste buds. If you want your readers to visualize a scene, if you want your characters to come alive, your settings to become more vivid, give them the scents, the feelings, the taste. Two lovers kissing, tasting sweat on each other's lips; an old house which smells of apples and pepper; the cold touch of the coins the paperboy gives you – we need to listen to the things we blank out because we consider them unimportant, thinking they're not the real matter of life and drama. But it *is* the real matter of life and drama, because it is life. A dog barking on a frosty winter night, rattling teaspoons in a coffee cup: this is the world. It's all part of the big picture: God, as Flaubert said, is in the details.

Heart

> It is only with the heart that one can see rightly; what is essential is invisible to the eye.
>
> *Antoine de St Exupéry*

The domain of literature is the domain of the heart. The communication being sought through fiction is an emotional one: pathos, excitement, laughter, fear – whatever. To communicate an emotion you have to experience the emotion in the first place. To expect your readers to be moved to tears at a scene which you wrote dry-eyed betrays either over-optimism or cold calculation on your part. Respect yourself, your readers and the creative act enough to give everything you have to it. It may not be easy – it will certainly be scary at times. But so far, no writer has died of fear.

Having a big heart means having a sense of humour and compassion, qualities which mark the great from the mediocre. Why is humour important? Because a sense of the absurd can be an antidote to any amount of self-important posturing. (But beware of trying to be funny: the laboured pun is a painful thing). Compassion? If we do laugh, it's through tears.

Who we are is important, the depths we allow ourselves to express makes a difference to the quality of our writing. We can never completely hide behind our words because our writing is, to recall Strunk and White, 'nondetachable'. The hand that holds the pen is attached to the arm, the arm to the body, the body to the spirit. And a mean spirit can be sniffed out by a reader, as can the opposite.

> The only way to become a better writer is to become a better person.
>
> *Brenda Ueland*

Muscle

What do I mean by 'muscle'? Strength and stamina. You need to be strong because to do a good job requires facing the demons of fear, laziness, your past, your future. The demons make for interesting reading, if we can but face them. The German poet

Rainer Maria Rilke put it this way: 'Our deepest fears are like dragons guarding our deepest treasure.' Once we push past the dragon we can access the riches of our imagination. This takes muscle.

> If you have a skeleton in your closet, take it out and dance with it.
>
> *Carolyn Mackenzie*

Stamina is needed because few people will be in the margins cheering you on – and even if they are, you're always alone when it comes to uncapping your pen. The writing of a novel is an emotional marathon; even if it is full of wonder and excitement, it is a long way to run.

Creating anything which has personal meaning requires an act of courage. In the moment of creativity we open ourselves to judgement and rejection. There are some things you can do to en-courage yourself which we'll look at in Chapter 13; however, the main thing is *trust*. Trust yourself, trust your thoughts and emotions, trust the universe, trust your readers. Your holding back from the page will make itself known to readers, perhaps without their conscious knowledge, but some part of them will sense your reluctance. A good story, they might say, but not brilliant – the author was nowhere to be seen.

Not holding back means inhabiting the text, being there with your characters, feeling what they are feeling, abandoning yourself to the creative moment. This, again, takes muscle.

> If you really want to achieve Greatness, you have to keep challenging yourself. You have to keep going back into yourself.
>
> *James Ellroy*

Voice

There is something beneath style, which I call 'voice'. A writer can have a different style for each novel, a style perhaps determined by the subject matter, but a single voice. We all have different voices, some more pleasant to listen to than others – the important thing is to use *your* voice, not that of somebody else. Speak with authority, declare yourself on the page: our writerly vocal cords can develop with practice.

> Talent alone cannot make a writer. There must be a man behind the book.
>
> *Ralph Waldo Emerson*

Related to this is the idea of honesty. By 'honesty' I simply mean not pretending knowledge that is not yours. Conspicuous learning will probably alienate most readers, arrogance will finish off the remainder. Humility is not false modesty, neither does it mean holding back from expressing yourself, rather it is the knowledge of your own fallibility. Resist the temptation to appropriate others' learning. Make your own discoveries and speak them with your own voice: simplicity and straightforwardness have a lot going for them. If you try to show off or seek to impress, your readers will smell a rat. Many apprentice writers struggle and strain to be clever or literary; few readers are fooled.

> The most essential gift for a good writer is a built-in, shockproof shit detector.
>
> *Ernest Hemingway*

A mind capable of aesthetic judgement

Innocent perception and stamina and strong vocal cords are not everything. Speaking your truth boldly and authentically may attract our attention and warm our hearts, but you must be saying something if you want to hold the reader's attention. Therefore you need to develop your powers of thinking if you are to grow beyond a certain point.

Isn't it enough to just tell a story? Yes. Then why develop our thinking? Because writing is not about writing. Consider it: writing is the end product of a process of thought. If writing was truly about the words on the page, then the most admired writers would be those with the largest vocabularies, or those with the best copperplate handwriting. Good writers are, in fact, good thinkers. Uh-oh, I hear. Not only do I have to be an artist, I have to be a philosopher.

Not true – intelligence isn't the same as intellect. The thinking of the novelist is done with organs other than the brain: the gut, or the spleen, or the heart for instance. Of course, the brain is important, but for once it isn't king, queen and knave. Intuition and imagination – the jokers in the pack – are of equal power in the mind of the novelist. Develop these qualities in yourself: grow into your writing, learning more about yourself, other people, and the world with every sentence you write.

The importance of considerateness

The beginning and end of writing is communication. This means finding a common language which can bridge the gulf between writer and reader. You won't manage this unless you can somehow put yourself in the shoes of the reader. The purpose of editing is taking the measure of your reader's foot: asking the imaginary reader in your mind a series of questions. Does this make sense? Could I use another, less obscure expression? Do the ideas match up? Have I given enough information?

A good writer is someone who cares for his readers enough not to be lazy, or wilfully obscure.

> I mean it when I say that a writer has to love his readers. You treat your readers as your children. You want to give them a good time and you want them to have inspiring and interesting thoughts.
>
> *Martin Amis*

Giving yourself away

There is a paradox in writing novels: you express yourself by giving yourself away. Unless you fully declare yourself, your work will have no authority, but if you declare yourself to the exclusion of the reader, the result will be boring, self-obsessed, inaccessible. You must always remember your reader, for if you don't, you'll be talking to yourself. Jean-Paul Sartre called writing an act of generosity between author and reader, and so it is. The writer gives care and effort and the temptation to self-indulgence; the reader gives a willing suspension of disbelief, time and effort.

> The progress of an artist is a continual self-sacrifice, a continuing extinction of personality.
>
> *T. S. Eliot*

Self-sacrifice means cutting out your favourite passages that contribute nothing to the story; it means editing again and again; it means holding back your opinions. The writer who is interested only in himself will be interesting only to himself.

This generosity of spirit does not mean there is a requirement for nobility: some of our best novelists have been famously misanthropic, opinionated, cruel even. It does mean, however, that everything is subjugated to the importance of the art: one's cherished opinions, approval of others, earning a living, even – some might say – one's health.

The writer's only responsibility is to his art. He will be completely ruthless if he is a good one ... If a writer has to rob his mother he will not hesitate; the *Ode to a Grecian Urn* is worth any number of old ladies.

William Faulkner

Things to try

1 Pause a moment wherever you are. Spend the next five minutes just absorbing the sights and sounds and smells around you. Then write for ten minutes beginning: 'At the moment . . .' Remember – be specific, be concrete.

2 List the things you want to communicate to other people (whether you actually will or not). They might be specific events from your past, or specific thoughts and feelings; they might be general thoughts and feelings.

3 Spend the next few minutes writing a list of your personal taboo subjects: topics you tell yourself you shouldn't write about. This exercise may be particularly useful if you don't want to do it. Now, spend ten minutes writing about one of your taboo subjects. *Courage, mon brave!*

support

In this chapter you will learn:
- the factors to consider when deciding where and when to write including the importance of solitude for a writer
- about sources of support – writers' circles, courses and books
- how to overcome writer's block.

Even writing at full steam ahead, a novel is likely to take six months' work. Few of us write with the wind in our hair for more than a few pages at a time, and the journey to that triumphant terminus THE END is more likely to take a couple of years. A long haul, certainly, and a journey with no shortage of bleached bones by the wayside, for patience and doggedness are qualities with limits. What can we do to make this journey easier, to feed us along the way so we do not have to draw solely on our own resources? In other words: how can we support ourselves? If we are serious about writing, we can check out our writing environment, enhancing those aspects which support us and jettisoning those which hold us back.

Our physical environment

What about a writing room, somewhere we can spread our papers, put our feet up, let our imagination go wild? Somewhere with DO NOT DISTURB written on the door. Although we may fantasize about such things, it isn't necessary to have an expensive desk and an ergonomic chair and a view of a lake in order to write well – more novels have been scribbled in exercise books at kitchen tables than in book-lined studios. As long as we have a chair which is not too uncomfortable, a flat surface to rest our page on and a pen which doesn't blot too much, our basic writing needs are met.

The *idea*, however, of a special, perhaps sanctified place for writing, is valuable. Putting aside an area of your living space for your writing will show yourself and the world that you intend to be taken seriously. Recognizing the importance of writing for yourself and declaring it to other people will help establish it in your life. After all, if you don't declare yourself as a writer, nobody else will.

If you have the luxury of a spare room, make its sole purpose that of writing. Keep your desk free of the clutter of everyday life, the unpaid bills and old magazines. This is *your* space: defend it against the rising tide of other demands. People might resent you for this, feeling jealous, accusing you of selfishness and self-indulgence. Hold your ground and growl at anyone who enters your lair.

If, like most people, you need to share your space, you can still make it your own when you are writing. Clear away the laundry from the table, adjust the seating and lighting to suit yourself.

Make a ritual of it: the physical preparation of writing can be an important part of the mental preparation. Again, growl at anyone who approaches, at least in the allocated time of your work. I am at work, you can tell them, and this is my office.

Time

It is of little use if we have a perfect writing environment and don't spend time there. Few people can devote as much time to writing as they would like – if this is the case, you will need to clear your diary just as you clear your desk. Free time will rarely come knocking at our door. You must make the time if you're serious about writing.

A large part of a writer's job looks like doing nothing: gazing out of the window, scribbling ideas on the backs of envelopes, writing words down and then crossing them out. It is easy to bow to the pressures – from ourselves and others – to do something productive instead. You will successfully make time for yourself, and defend it against other demands, only if you believe you are worth it.

Things you should know

There will only ever be 24 hours in a day
If you find yourself too busy to write, you will have to prioritize, cutting some things out in order to make space for writing. It may help if you tell yourself that self-expression is a *need*, not a luxury. Left to determine your own priorities, it is easy to place writing at the bottom of the list. See if you can elevate it a bit: the busy mother, the overworked executive, the burdened student – we all must find time for ourselves if we are to have full psychic health.

Even ten minutes is long enough to write
If you think it isn't worth sitting down to write unless you have a free afternoon, think again. It may be frustrating to stop before you're ready, but at least you'll have something to show for your frustration. If you don't write, you won't even have that – just the frustration.

> Write as often as possible, not with the idea at once of getting into print, but as if you were learning an instrument.
>
> *J. B. Priestley*

You don't need pen and paper to write

Words are the end of the process, not the beginning. The start of writing is in the domain of ideas, and this can be done at any time and any place. A friend of mine spends 45 minutes driving to work – an hour and a half every day, seven and a half hours per week – time that he uses to plan his stories and get to know his characters. I haven't asked him, but I suppose he welcomes traffic jams when the work is going well. My most creative time is before I go to sleep at night – a pencil and piece of paper is all I need in case inspiration strikes. In the bath, on your daily walk, washing up – use any routine activity for your writing. You don't even have to tell people what you're doing.

Writers, so far as I can see, never have holidays. Once the process of becoming a writer is under way you can't stop it. Once you have begun, everything in the world is filtered through your writer's perception.

Hilary Mantel

Skill comes with practice

The more you write, the more you will find words doing your bidding and the less time you will spend scratching your head. This involves discipline, however, and not only writing just when you feel like it. You might not be able to turn inspiration on and off like a tap, but we can all set our alarm clocks half an hour early.

Discipline is the refining fire by which talent becomes ability.

Roy L Smith

People

Writing a novel is a solitary activity. It is done in quiet moments, away from other people. The cauldron within which ideas bubble is not open for public inspection – it is just ourselves and the page. The freedom to disappear into the imaginative world, live for a moment-out-of-time away from the constraints of the real world; this is why I write, why many people write. A certain detachment is necessary to fully take flight, for unless we let go of the real world, we cannot enter the other world. Solitude – either physically living alone and writing alone, or for the moment of writing having no intrusions into your privacy – is an essential component of the creative act. Solitude has a cost however: loneliness.

Loneliness, the sweet-sour feeling of separateness, may not be a bad thing. However, when it turns in on itself to become despair and depression and alienation, then we may find ourselves in trouble, for it will probably dry the ink in our pens. If you recognize this in yourself, find some company, talk to your friends until you find someone who will take you seriously. Enrol sympathetic people into your project. You don't need to give them much detail – in fact, at first, keep your storyline to yourself. Tell them whatever you think is enough so that you can celebrate triumphs with them and commiserate over defeats. Though nobody can hold the pen for you, there is no need to go it alone.

Writers' circles, courses and books

A second tier of support is that of the writers' circle. Every group is different – some meet in hired halls, others in member's homes. Some charge annual fees, others are more informal. Most towns have writers' circles – try your local library for their addresses. The advantages are plain: like-minded people who can offer not only support, but informed feedback.

Writing a novel, however, is rarely a collaborative process, so beware of too much feedback. It is *your* novel, after all, and for you to write in your way.

Creative writing courses, either run by local education authorities or privately run, are worth exploring if you want to spend time with other writers. The more substantial courses are run either as activity holidays (for instance, on the Greek island of Skyros), or as week-long residentials in the countryside (The Arvon Foundation and Fen Farm are both very popular) or as non-residential one- or two-day courses. The range in hours, cost and level covers the whole spectrum – look in the writing press or libraries for details.

Books, said the philosopher Alan Watts, are the modern gurus. And so they are: few apprentice writers have the opportunity to meet experienced writers, and so their words on the page come in useful. The number of books on creative writing is burgeoning, and it is sometimes hard to separate the good from the mediocre. A bibliography of recommended reading is at the back of this book.

Writing a novel is not the same as talking about writing a novel, or studying to write a novel, or reading how to write a novel. Don't get these confused.

Writer's block

Regardless of experience or track record, it is inevitable that sooner or later you will grind to a halt in your novel. Hopefully the stalled engine is temporary, just a matter of recharging the battery for a while. Sometimes the condition is more serious: the dreaded writer's block.

There are two types of writer's block: technical and non-technical. Technical writer's block is often the easier of the two to deal with: this is just a matter of doing more research so that you can maintain credibility in the story, or deepening your understanding of your characters so they come alive, or plotting more thoroughly so you can proceed in the telling.

Non-technical writer's block is the result of something other than the story. If this is the case, trying to find the solution on the page is rarely the best approach. Sometimes being a writer means leaving your desk and going outside to chop wood, or bursting into tears of frustration, or sitting down and asking yourself questions.

Physical blocks

Sometimes our physical environment is at odds with the creative process. A computer that refuses to do our bidding, the noise of the stereo from upstairs, physical aches and pains – these can all be effective blocks. Rather than trying to ignore the interference, deal with it. It might mean forking out for a good chair, or writing in the library. It might mean cutting coffee out of your diet, or exercising before you sit down to work. Your brain does not operate independently of your body: trying to work after a heavy meal might be counter-productive, as may working at the end of a hard day. Thinking burns calories – sometimes you may want to write, but your body is just too tired. You are not a brain on a stick, remember.

Emotional blocks

Emotional blocks are caused by locking in feelings which demand to be let out – a kind of emotional constipation. Self-expression is *self*-expression, rather than self-*expression*: writing asks that you bring the whole of yourself to the page, and this includes those feelings you would rather leave unacknowledged. There is a place for appropriate expression – becoming an artist doesn't mean going wild and disregarding other people. However, it does mean recognizing the legitimacy of your feelings.

Psychological blocks

Psychological blocks are the result of negative beliefs of long standing. These beliefs fall into two camps: beliefs we know about; beliefs we don't know about. If we are aware of the negative beliefs, we're halfway to solving it, for at least we know where the hand brake is. If we are unaware of the beliefs holding us back, we will smell burning rubber and not know where it comes from.

The first step in mastery over our blocks is in being aware of them. In terms of our negative beliefs, this means getting them out in the open where we can see them. Like little squirmy things that live under rocks, our negative beliefs don't like the light of day: they are at home in the dark where they are unchallenged. Once your negative beliefs are out in the open, the second step is to rigorously examine their truthfulness. They will seem true, after all that is why they are causing you problems – some part of you is believing them. However, are they *really* true? Only you can tell. Some perennial favourites you might recognize:

I've got no imagination	– Try looking at your dreams if you think this is true.
I'm not intelligent enough	– What does 'enough' mean? Anyway, where is the rule which says you need to be intelligent to be a good writer?
It's not safe to express myself	– Just because you have been hurt in the past, does that mean it will inevitably happen again?
I'm not good enough	– If there was somebody else with exactly the same qualities as yourself, would you dismiss them thus? If not, what gives you the right to judge yourself by different criteria?

Ignoring blocks – whatever their source – can be a time-consuming business. Sitting at your desk chewing a pencil, or not even making it to your desk, can spin the writing of a novel out for year after tedious year. Sometimes problems resolve themselves on their own; the chances, however, are that they will be resolved by giving up writing.

Some unblocking techniques

If you are faced with a stalled engine rather than an all-out breakdown these techniques may be enough to get you started.

Brainstorming

If you are overwhelmed with the project ahead of you, not knowing where to start, try free-associating ideas, putting down anything in any order. Use a lot of plain (not lined) paper for this – give your ideas room to breathe. Also avoid writing linearly: corralling your thoughts may be part of the problem. Put your hand in your pocket and pull out whatever ideas may be there, scatter them on the paper – you can assess their viability later. You can develop this technique further into what is called 'clustering' or 'branching'. (See the bibliography for books on these techniques.)

Write with your non-dominant hand

This means your left hand if you are normally right-handed and vice versa. Take a few minutes to have a written dialogue between your positive self (expressed with your non-dominant hand) and your negative self (your dominant hand). Begin the discussion with your positive voice having its say, and then give your negative voice its say, explaining why it is blocking you. Continue the discussion, passing the pen back and forth between both hands until you reach a natural end. Be sure to finish the dialogue with the positive voice having the final word.

Sabotage page

When you are working, have a separate sheet of paper beside you. Whenever any negative thoughts come up which are sabotaging your free flow, write them down. There is no need to deal with them – like fractious children demanding attention, it is sometimes enough just to acknowledge their existence.

End the day in the middle of a scene

Maintaining momentum is an important part of the novel writing process. If you always have trouble getting going, leave an unfinished idea for you to return to – even an unfinished sentence may be enough. Having something to start with can be enough to turn the engine over so that the cylinders fire.

Write your favourite scene

If you are stuck on a particular scene, leave it and go on to a scene which you are confident of, returning when you feel ready. There is no rule which says you have to eat your greens before you can start on the pudding.

Remind yourself why you want to write

If your enthusiasm flags it often shows on the page. If it dries up completely it won't show on the page except as white space. Write a list of all the reasons why you want to write this book. Talk to people about the book. Refuse to listen to any negative thoughts about it – believe in yourself.

Give yourself a break

If all else fails – and sometimes it does – leave your writing and do something different, preferably physical. Go for a walk, cook something, mow the lawn. Give your brain a rest, and don't think about the project. Like trying to remember a forgotten word, not thinking about your novel may bring ideas to mind that you were having trouble accessing. Keep an eye on this, however, just to make sure it doesn't topple over into procrastinating.

Writing as an organic process

Sometimes the reason your writing refuses to budge is not because you are blocked but because the idea isn't ready. Like a seed in winter, your novel may be biding its time. Yes, there are deadlines for some of us, yes our time may be limited, yes we may really want to write the story, but neither the novel nor the human imagination are mechanical things. Just as there is a time for a seed to germinate, so too there is a time for ideas. If your idea is not ready, keep it watered and warm, check at intervals to see if anything is sprouting – but don't force its growth. It may take months for your idea to be ready, years even. If you are in a hurry to get ahead, try another idea which may be ready. If you go ahead regardless, your novel may be like a winter tomato – suspiciously wan and tasteless.

Things to try

1 Assess your writing environment. What does it say about the place of writing in your life? What *do* you want to say? What changes could you make to reflect your wants?

2 The next time you are blocked, take a piece of paper and list all the negative beliefs you have about the project. Then, one by one, verify their truthfulness. If most of them are false, or imponderable, what *is* the truth?

3 Affirmations are statements which declare the very best of yourself and life. Find an affirming statement which fits for you and write it where you can see it regularly. Some examples: I have a limitless imagination; I have the right to express myself; it is safe to take chances with my writing. If you repeat these regularly, and with sufficient sincerity, they will become a part of your thinking. If you need any evidence that the way we think affects our writing, try repeating again and again 'My writing is dull and lifeless' before you sit down to work. Although pessimists may think they are being realistic, their beliefs are no less subjective than an optimist's. Given the choice between two imponderables – between, say, 'I *can* do it', and 'I *can't* do it', I know which I would rather choose to believe.

4 At the start of each day, assess the day's commitments, and then allocate a slot of time (at least ten minutes) in which you will write – come what may.

5 Reward yourself for reaching deadlines – doing so shows you take your writing seriously, and encourages you to continue doing so. The carrot usually works better than the stick.

marketing

In this chapter you will learn:
- the pros and cons of approaching publishers yourself or engaging an agent to represent you
- about self-publishing and vanity publshing
- how to present your manuscript to a publisher
- the process from submission of a manuscript through to publication
- the likely financial arrangement you will have with your publisher.

When students ask me how to approach publishers, I always ask one question first: have you written the book? Rarely do they answer in the affirmative. Unless you have an idea of such burning originality, or a title of such irresistibility (although it is hard to see how this could be the case with a novel), or a proven track record as a novelist, or just happen to be famous, the most a publisher will says is: 'Sounds interesting – let me see it when it's finished.' A writer, remember, is someone who writes.

When you have finished your novel – edited it, redrafted it, shown it to informed friends – then what? There are two main routes to a publisher: going it alone, and via an agent.

Going it alone

If you decide to approach publishers yourself, it will pay to do your homework. There is no point sending your space-opera novella to a religious publisher, your sex-and-shopping book to Mills and Boon: publishers have lists, outside of which they rarely stray. Enticing a publisher into a new area on the strength of your writing alone is unlikely to happen.

The best way of studying a publisher's list is by getting hold of their catalogue. See who they publish, what types of fiction. Could they offer your book a home? If you can't get a catalogue, hang around your local bookshop (most libraries are too poorly stocked with new books to be worth consulting) and note the imprints of books similar to your own. There is no shortage of publishers – many of them are subsidiaries of a couple of handfuls of big companies. Find their addresses in a directory such as the *Writer's and Artists Yearbook* (published yearly by A and C Black). If your book is good enough, it will find a home. It's just a matter of looking.

Once you have targeted your publisher, write a *brief* letter saying who you are, including any information you think is relevant (previous publishing triumphs only count if they are substantial – fillers and published letters won't impress an editor). Publishers of fiction often see their investment in authors rather than books, for few first novels earn anything more than enough to cover costs. The second or third or fourth book from the same author will hopefully see greater returns. If a publisher thinks this will be a one-off (and most first-time novelists never go on to write a second), they may not be easily persuaded to invest in your book. You don't have to have a degree in English Literature, but you do need to demonstrate a commitment to a career as a novelist. If you're unsure of your vocation, keep your doubts to yourself.

Included with the letter, on a separate sheet, you should write a synopsis of your novel in about two or three hundred words. Lastly, include a couple of sample chapters. Send this lot off, and then wait. If you haven't heard anything after a month or so, follow it up with a letter. Publishers are often very slow, but in my experience, they are thorough. Your proposal, or – if they request it – the whole manuscript, will be assessed thoroughly. Everybody, after all, is looking for the next bestseller.

Agents

Writers fall into two camps – those who think agents are invaluable, and those who don't. If you are a beginner, particularly if you prefer writing to networking, an agent could make the difference between being published and not. Some well-known authors represent themselves, enjoying the autonomy of going it alone – it's a matter of choice.

The agent is popularly caricatured either as a rapacious conman who might as well be selling mobile phones as books, or a hero of the downtrodden writer, ready to lend them a tenner in times of need, available to be called in the middle of the night when writer's block strikes. Neither of these is true in my experience. An agent – a good agent – is part business partner, part gentle stoker of the author's fires of industry, and – hopefully – someone whose company you enjoy. An agent's job is *not* to write the book; if you are lucky, and if you request it, they will offer editorial advice. An agent's job *is*: to find a publisher for your book, trawl through the small print of the contract to make sure you have the best available deal, and keep your name alive when people have forgotten who you are. And this they do for 10 per cent (sometimes 12$\frac{1}{2}$ per cent, occasionally 15 per cent) of the earnings of each book they represent. Some authors resent the giving away of a proportion of their income; however, 90 per cent of something is better than 100 per cent of nothing.

How to find an agent? If you have writer friends with agents, personal recommendations count for a lot – both for you in choosing someone who is suitable, and, if your contact speaks to his agent, yourself as a prospective client. Otherwise, look in one of the directories (see under Recommended reading). How to approach an agent? In the same way as a publisher – personal letter, synopsis, sample chapters. Will I automatically be accepted by an agent? No. Finding an agent is perhaps easier than finding a publisher, however, getting a good agent is far from guaranteed – they will only take on an author if they are confident of an eventual sale. So, will having an agent automatically mean my book will be taken? (This is a rhetorical question.) Your manuscript arriving at a publishers with the recommendations of a reputable agent will mean it gets seen sooner rather than later, and if rejected will likely be done politely and personally. An unagented manuscript will probably fester on the so-called slush pile until the office has a clear out, and if rejected will likely be done with a standard letter. Photocopied slips are not unknown. Publishers *are* human beings with feelings and not monsters, we have to remind ourselves at times – they are just very busy. A large publishing house might receive thousands of unsolicited manuscripts a year.

Rejections happen more often than acceptance – if reasons for rejection are given, take note, though unless the letter was very encouraging don't rewrite the book and try again. Even though commissioning editors should have a good eye for a saleable book, they cannot be anything other than subjective. The changes you might make could spoil it for another editor.

> If a publisher declines your manuscript, remember it is merely the decision of one fallible human being, and try another.
>
> *Stanley Unwin*

There have been some famously poor editorial judgements: *Catch 22, Watership Down, Kinflicks, The Celestine Prophesy* – all were rejected 20, 30, 40 times, now all are bestsellers. If you believe in your book, persist.

Self-publishing and vanity publishing

Writers of note – from Mark Twain to Timothy Mo – have, for various reasons, published their own books. The obvious advantage of doing so is the guarantee that, if nothing else, you will become a published novelist within your lifetime. You will have total editorial control, and within the laws of copyright and libel, the freedom to print whatever you like. Any profit is yours – and the tax collector's.

The route to self-publication, notwithstanding the obstacles, is well trodden: if you want to explore the possibility, be well informed. There are many books on the subject, and an increasing number of courses which can guide you in making a success of it. It *is* possible, for relatively low outgoings, to be a published author. Printing the book, however, is often the easy part – in order to cover your costs you will have to print several thousand. Unless you want to insulate your loft with copies of your novel, you will have to sell them – this means marketing. Persuading enough bookshops to order copies of a book from an unknown author and an unknown imprint is no small challenge. André Gide had to shred almost all copies of his first book when he failed to sell them. It was probably an excellent book – but good writers rarely have good business acumen.

So-called vanity publishing is a form of self-publication in which the author pays a company – a publisher only in name – in a spurious partnership in which all the costs and risk are borne by the author. Such companies often purport to give informed advice about the quality of any work you send them, assuring you of your skill and the likelihood of this book selling well. Once they have your money, no attempt to market your book will be made. It is not a cheap way to have your book badly printed and packaged. Far better to go it alone.

> No matter what you do to please the editors, it will never please them. Better please yourself and trust in God. So many good men had to print their own books for themselves at first. Walt Whitman peddled his own book from door to door.
>
> *Lawrence Durrell*

Presenting your manuscript to a publisher

When you send your manuscript through the post to a publisher (or deliver it by hand), include your name and address on the first and last page, just in case it parts company from your letter. Also, always keep duplicates of your work – hefty typescripts do go missing. Jilly Cooper left her only copy of a manuscript on a bus, and never got it back. A bag containing my fourth book was snatched from an editor in New York by a mugger – luckily I had the original on computer disc.

The convention of the presentation of manuscripts is as follows:

- typed or word processed on A4 paper
- wide margins on top and bottom and either side (for editorial remarks)
- double spacing between lines (meaning an average of about 25–30 lines per page)
- one side of the paper only
- number the pages (just in case somebody drops it)
- avoid a poor quality, dot-matrix print-out which is hard to read
- likewise a worn-out typewriter ribbon
- do not bind or staple the pages – editors and printers prefer to handle each folio separately.

A good many young writers make the mistake of enclosing a stamped, self-addressed envelope, big enough for the manuscript to come back in. This is too much of a temptation to the editor.

Ring Lardner

Regardless of what Ring Lardner says, including the return postage will ensure you see your work again, if that is what you want.

The key to presentation is legibility: you want to give the person who reads it as easy a time as possible so they can get on with the story. If you are sending out the manuscript yourself, keep an eye on how dog-eared it is getting: a well-thumbed manuscript will tell the reader he or she isn't the first to tread this way. Sending good quality photocopies is acceptable; but avoid carbon copies which smudge and are fuzzy. Also, although it isn't a spelling test, misspelt words will send a signal which will not be in your favour.

Publishers are professionals – they expect to be treated as such. If you are an undiscovered genius, perhaps one day somebody will steer their way through the ink blots and spelling errors to declare their find to the world. It may, however, be a long wait.

Most authors would consider it undesirable to approach a publisher in a dirty and incoherent condition. But that is, in effect, what they do when they submit a dirty and dilapidated manuscript.

Stanley Unwin

From presentation to publication

When you submit your manuscript it will likely join a heap waiting for someone to sort and sift before it topples over – the so-called slush pile. The someone is usually either the editorial department junior (i.e. under 25) or an old hand who comes in a couple of mornings a week and is paid by the hour. In either case they are basically on your side and keen to discover something good – the junior to make his or her name and acquire an author of their own if they are lucky, the old hand to justify continuing freelance employment.

If they think your novel is promising they will pass it on to a more senior editor and eventually it will surface at an acquisitions meeting. The championing editor will not only have to justify accepting your novel on grounds of intrinsic merit and potential sales, but also say whether you as an author seem to be a continuing property (which you will have assured them in your letter). Also the question is raised of how promotable you are likely to be – an important factor in an age when a new novel needs all the help it can get. To this end, publishers often like to meet a potential author before clinching the offer.

The next step is the longed-for phone call offering to publish it (or if there are significant changes to be made, suggesting a meeting in which they can be discussed). An advance against royalties will be offered, that is, a lump sum to be paid, usually in three or four instalments: the first on signing a contract, the second on final acceptance of the manuscript, the third on hardback publication and the fourth, up to one year later, on appearance of the paperback. This is a non-refundable advance – in other words, a fee which will be set against hoped-for future sales of your book. This is all the money you will see unless or until your percentage of the total sales (usually 10 per cent of the cover price of the book) reaches the advanced amount. If this happens, then you will begin earning your ten per cent – the proportion rising to about 15 per cent after your sales pass certain agreed-upon milestones. If your sales never reach that amount, you don't have to return any unearned advance.

Once you have accepted their terms and signed a contract there will probably be a wait of up to a year before your book hits the shops. Printing and packaging a book can be done swiftly if necessary; for most novels however, there is no hurry, so your novel will join an orderly queue and be released when it stands its best chance of getting some attention from the press and public.

Meanwhile two important stages have still to be passed: the proofs and the cover. When the final manuscript has been accepted, it will be typeset and then returned to you for checking. This is not the time to rewrite the book: it is for you to check for typographical errors, and make minor alterations. Most contracts will contain a clause stating that if more than 10 per cent of the typeset text needs to be changed, the author must pay the typesetting fee. Due to the nature of typesetting, however, this does not mean you can change one word in ten.

Few contracts give the author any say about the presentation of the book; however, the more reputable publishers will at least consult the author before going ahead with commissioning a cover, likewise the blurb (the synopsis of the story on the inside cover) and author biography (usually inside the back cover).

During this time the marketing department will have moved into action, including the book in its catalogue, informing the sales force about its appearance. Uncorrected proofs of the book will be sent out to the national press with the hope they will review it when it is released. Advertising space in the newspapers will be booked if you are lucky. Relevant and famous people will be sent copies in the hope they will praise it lavishly, and their comments included on the cover.

Then, finally, the launch date looms. Few novelists are afforded launch parties, or have the press clamouring at their door, so don't expect too much. The world hasn't been waiting with baited breath for your book – but *you* have. There are many victories along the novelist's way: seeing your novel in the shops is the greatest of them all. Enjoy every last thrilling drop of emotion of seeing your creation realized.

And then come the reviews. Whatever they say, remember: this is just one person's opinion.

> Asking a working writer what he thinks about critics is like asking a lamp-post how he feels about dogs.
>
> *Christopher Hampton*

Money

There is lots of money to be made by writing fiction – just as there is lots to be made in any industry. The top bestsellers, we must realize, are a tiny fraction of the whole field. Most writers, even very well-known writers, only dream of sales in the hundreds of thousands. Occasionally we hear of enormous advances for first novels; however, the standard amount is between £2,000 and £6,000. We may complain about the returns for our effort – the long hours and pitiful pay and the publishers getting fat on our labour – but as the joke goes, at least it beats working for a living.

Most novelists do not support themselves through full-time fiction writing: teaching, reviewing, working in advertising or publishing – novelists skirt the periphery of writing if they can, but there are as many writers working outside these fields as there are resting actors serving tables.

Genre fiction

The money an author earns generally reflects sales (not always: top-flight literary figures often don't 'earn out' their advances). Sales in fiction reflect the public's appetite for genre: thrillers, sagas, romance, fantasy and horror generally sell better than 'literary', non-genre fiction. If you decide to write genre fiction do it for two reasons before you think of the money: first, because you have always read it, like reading it still, and will probably continue to read it; second, because you like writing it. A cynical approach will probably show – genre alone will not generate many sales: if you want to break out of the almost-rans into the first division, you must do something interesting with the form.

> Genre is merely the clothing a novel may wear. For lesser writers, admittedly, the clothing may be all there is: what you see is what you get. But, for the great masters of genre fiction, the clothing is merely a disguise.
>
> *Alan Massie*

Genres indicate trends which may last for years, sub-genres indicate fashions which are far more ephemeral. Having your thumb on the commercial pulse is useful if you write such specific fiction, though again, no guarantee an editor will be interested. For an outsider, the most interesting things about sub-genres are often their names: sex and shopping, aga sagas, bodice-rippers, women in jeopardy, space opera, star dreck.

Write for love, publish for money

For most of us, money is a distraction to the creative process: not having money, however, is even more of a distraction. So, publish for money, by all means, but write for love. If you don't, it will surely tell, for there is no hiding our motivation from the perceptive reader: each word on the page is a mirror of our intention – hidden or not. If your first goal is to be published, such ambition will likely taint what you are writing, and ironically reduce your chances of a sale. With the growing competition to secure a reader's attention (8,000 new novels are published each year in Britain – and rising) originality and chance-taking counts for a lot, qualities you are unlikely to manifest if you are thinking too hard of a market.

The logical conclusion of worrying about commercial viability, or slotting into the market, or the profile of your subject, is the reduction of the novel to a commodity whose literary worth is measured in terms of poundage (or more probably, ounces). Reaching readers is important – perhaps vital if we are to continue; making a living is also necessary. There is something else, however, some mysterious quality beyond the reach of the market and the critic – the integrity of the creative act. Write for nothing and no-one first of all. Write because you must. Write because there is a truth which demands to be burnt onto paper. Write in the face of your lethargy and despair and doubts. Write because you don't know how to write, because you don't know what you believe.

Then write for yourself, for the pleasure it gives you. Write because you love language, because you love fantasy, because you love the freedom of creating a world beyond the reach of others.

Only *then* write for other people. Some writers find it useful to imagine their ideal reader listening to their words as they are being written; others (myself included) have only the vaguest idea of an audience. But whether defined or abstract, the reader should be someone you love and respect – a person who has the piercing vision to see through any pretence surrounding your work.

Then think about editors and publishers and critics.

> My whole theory of writing I can sum up in one sentence. An author ought to write for the youth of his own generation, the critics of the next, and the schoolmasters of ever afterward.
>
> *F. Scott Fitzgerald*

taking it further

Recommended reading

There are many books relevant to the fiction writer. Here are some I have found particularly useful:

Aristotle *On the Art of Poetry*, published as *Classical Literary Criticism*, Penguin Classics, 1965. Literary theory stripped to the bone. Essential reading, if only to disagree with it.

Allott, Miriam *Novelists on the Novel*, Routledge and Kegan Paul, 1959. A compendium of quotations from novelists about all aspects of novel writing. Out of print now, but worth tracking a copy down.

Boylan, Clare (ed.), *The Agony and the Ego*, Penguin Books, 1993. Essays by contemporary fiction writers.

Braine, John *Writing a Novel*, Methuen, 1974. Author of *Room at the Top*: stern and authoritative advice based on years of experience.

Brande, Dorothea *Becoming a Writer*, Macmillan, 1996. Perhaps the most loved book on creative writing. First published in 1934, its inspirational and insightful message is still going strong. Valuable writing exercises to get you started – foreword by Malcolm Bradbury.

Cappacchione, Lucia *The Power of the Other Hand*, Newcastle, 1988. 'Clustering' exercises as a way into your store of inspiration.

Casterton, Julia *Creative Writing*, Macmillan, 1986. Practical, intelligent and humane.

Doubtfire, Dianne *The Craft of Novel-Writing*, Allison and Busby, 1978. *Creative Writing*, Hodder and Stoughton, 1996. Thorough, no-nonsense advice with plenty of examples from texts.

Fairfax, John *Creative Writing*, Elm Tree Books, 1989.

Fairfax, John with John Moat, *The Way to Write*, Elm Tree Books, 1981. The founders of the Arvon Foundation: experienced poets both. Useful exercises.

Forster, E. M. *Aspects of the Novel*, Pelican Books, 1962. A collection of lectures delivered at Cambridge University in 1927. Fresh and unaffected, this book has become a classic. Invaluable chapters on plot and character.

Goldberg, Natalie *Writing Down the Bones*, Shambala, 1986. *Wild Mind*, Bantam, 1990. A Zen poetess and teacher of creative writing. The most inspirational writer on the subject that I know.

Kitchen, Paddy *The Way to Write Novels*, Elm Tree Books, 1981. Another Arvon tutor: a personal and approachable style.

Klauser, Henriette Anne *Writing on Both Sides of the Brain*, Harper and Row, 1986. Exercises on brainstorming techniques.

Lodge, David *The Art of Fiction*, Penguin Books, 1992. A fascinating collection of articles from *The Independent on Sunday*, useful for the reader as well as the writer.

Paris Review Interviews *Writers at Work*, (7 vols), Secker and Warburg and Penguin, 1958-85. An invaluable insight into the minds and working methods of successful writers.

Shaugnessy, Susan *Meditations for Writers,* Harper Collins, 1993. Affirmations and helpful quotes to keep you going.

Strunk, William and **E. B. White**, *The Elements of Style*, Macmillan, 1979. *The* book on style by two masters.

Ueland, Brenda *If you Want to Write*, Element Books, 1991. First published in 1938. Delightful and inspiring.

Wilson, Colin *The Craft of the Novel*, Gollancz, 1975. An interesting history of the development of the craft of the novel.

Reference books

Wells, Gordon *The Book Writer's Handbook*, Allison and Busby, 1989.

Allen, R. E. *The Oxford Writer's Dictionary*, Oxford University Press, 1990. Invaluable for those tricky questions of style and usage.

The Writer's Handbook, Papermac (published yearly). Almost every address you would ever need.

Writers' and Artists' Yearbook, A & C Black. Much the same as the above. Useful chapters on Finances, the Law, publishing practices, etc.

Books in Print to see if anyone has got there before you.

Writing courses

There has been a recent burgeoning of organizations which run writing courses. Here are five well-established ones with a high standard of tuition by professional writers:

The Arvon Foundation, Totley Barton, Sheep Wash, Beaworthy, Devon EX21 5NS, tel. 01409 231338. Has been running one-week residential courses since the late 1960s. They have three centres: Devon, Yorkshire and Inverness.

Fen Farm, Fen Road, Blo Norton, near Diss, Norfolk IP22 2JH, tel. 01379 898741. Offers residential writing courses in a 17th-century farmhouse.

International Forum Ltd, The Oast House, Plaxtol, Sevenoaks, Kent TN15 0QG, tel. 01732 810925. Although they cater mostly for screen-writers, their non-residential weekend courses are relevant for story tellers in any medium. They host Robert McKee's story structure course – a must for anyone struggling with plot problems.

Skyros Holistic Holidays, 92 Prince of Wales Road, London, NW5 3NE, tel. 0207 267 4424. Run two-week activity holidays on the Greek island of Skyros from April to October. Their recent writing holidays have attracted many well-known tutors.

Taliesin Trust, Ty Newydd, Llanystumdwy, Cricieth, Gwynedd LL52 0LW, tel. 01766 522811. A residential writers' centre in north Wales, running 4½-day and weekend courses from May to November.

index

abstract nouns **101**
adjectives **100**
adverbs **101**
agents **149–50**
allegory **43**
Amis, Kingsley **42, 135**
Amis, Martin **44**
antagonism, sources of **24**
archetypes **58–9**
arcs, grand, major and minor **32–3**
Aristotle **31, 36, 49, 115**
attributive verbs **71–2**
autobiography **62**

back story **121–2**
Barnes, Julian **43**
Barth, John **104**
Bradbury, Malcolm **61, 73**
Brande, Dorothea **129**
Buñuel, Luis **7**
Byatt, A. S. **10**

Calvino, Italo **103**
Camus, Albert **45, 119**
Cappachione, Lucia **129**
Carter, Angela **110**
Cary, Joyce **114**
Chagall, Marc **103**
characterisation versus character **52, 54, 55**
Christie, Agatha **37, 77**
chronology **117–18**
Churchill, Winston **109**
circumlocution **99**

Clavell, James **68**
clichés **102**
climax **30–1**
Cocteau, Jean **102**
Coleridge, S. T. **12, 29**
Collector, The **75, 78**
Colton, C. C. **99**
Comforts of Madness, The **22**
conflict **22, 23**
Conrad, Joseph **9, 43, 76**
critical choice **30**

Dahl, Roald **2, 24**
Danny The Champion of the World **24**
Death of a Salesman **44**
de St Exupéry, Antoine **132**
de Sousa, Steve **108**
dialect and foreign languages **68**
Dickens, Charles **44, 59**
dreams **4**
Duffy, Bruce **3**
du Maurier, Daphne **76**
Durrell, Lawrence **151**

Eliot, T. S. **xiii, 135**
Ellroy, James **133**
Emerson, Ralph Waldo **133**
empathy **50, 61**

Fatal Attraction **24**
Faulkner, William **136**
feedback **123, 125**
Fitzgerald, F. Scott **156**

Flaubert, Gustave **3, 97**
flashback **120–1**
focal length **94**
Ford, Ford Madox **94, 115**
Forster, E. M. **18, 19, 33, 49, 59, 62, 84, 120**
Fowler **99–100, 102**
Fowles, John **75, 78**
Frayn, Michael **7**

genre **17, 107, 155**
Goldberg, Natalie **91, 129**
Greene, Graham **61**

Hard Times **44**
Hardy, Thomas **63, 88, 103**
Heart of Darkness, The **43, 90**
Hemingway, Ernest **52, 63, 134**
Hesse, Herman **82–4, 119**
Highsmith, Patricia **6**
History of the World in 10½ Chapters, A **43**
Hubbard, Elbert **13**
Huxley, Aldous **62**

imagery **46, 101–2**

James, Henry **3, 49, 92**
John Thomas and Lady Jane **68**
Jong, Erica **128**
Joyce, James **73, 84–5**

Kafka, Franz **8**
Keneally, Thomas **10**
Kesey, Ken **43**
King Lear **42, 60–1**
King's English, The **99**

Lady Chatterley's Lover **37, 46**
Lawrence, D. H. **54, 62, 68, 92**
Lardner, Ring **152**
Lee, Laurie **98**
LeGuin, Ursula **16, 44, 53**
Life Game, The **85, 121**
Lodge, David **18, 45, 75**
Lolita **8**
Lord of the Rings, The **9**
Lucky Jim **42**
Lurie, Alison **118**

Mackenzie, Carolyn **133**
MacNeice, Louis **103**
Mantel, Hilary **140**
Massie, Alan **155**
McKee, Robert **25, 37, 55**
Metamorphosis **8**
metaphor **43–4, 101–2**
Michaels, Leonard **108**
money **154–6**
Money **44**
Mosquito Coast, The **58**
motivation of character **57**
multiple plots **42–3**
mystery **17**

names **44, 91–2**
narrative time **120–2**
Nostromo **9**
Nabokov, Vladimir **8**
Nineteen Eighty-Four **57**

One Flew over the Cuckoo's Nest **43, 44**
Orwell, George **57**
Outsider, The **45, 119**

pace **42, 118–9**
Passage to India, A **33, 120**
Picasso, Pablo **51**
Pliny the Younger **115**
plot, definition of **19**
Point Counter Point **62**
Porter, Katherine Anne **11**
Portrait of the Artist as a Young Man, A **83**
Priestley, J. B. **139**
Prodigy, The **83**
protagonist, single, dual and multiple **76**

qualifiers **101**
quest **21, 29**

Reade, Charles **17**
readiness, the point of **9**
Rebecca **76**
research **6–7**
resolution **23, 32**
Return of the Native **88**

reversal **31–2**
Rilke, Rainer Maria **133**
Rogers, Will **90**
roman à clef **61–3**
Romeo and Juliet **37, 76**
Rosa, João Guimaraes **89**
round and flat characters **59–60**

Sartre, Jean-Paul **22, 135**
Sayer, Paul **22**
self publishing **150–1**
sensibility **128–9**
sentimentality **102**
Shakespeare, William **60–61**
Shogun **68**
show, don't tell **93, 131**
simile **43–4, 101–2**
Simon, Danny **116**
Smith, Roy L. **140**
Sophie's Choice **28, 42, 88**
speech, conventions of written **73**
speech, three functions of **66–7**
speech, types of **70–3**
stasis **28**
Steinbeck, John **125**
Stendhal **100**
stereotypes **58, 59**
Stevenson, Robert Louis **72, 88**
Strunk and White **97, 101, 102**
Styron, William **28, 88**
subject matter **5, 107–8**
sub-text **68**
surprise **29, 31, 36**
suspense **17**
sympathy **50–1, 61**

tautology **99**
Theroux, Paul **58**
thesis **109–12**
thread **108–9**
title **45**
Tolkein, J. R. R. **9**
Tolstoy, Leo **112**
tone **84–5**
Townsend, Sue **2**
trigger **28**
Trollope, Anthony **65**
Twenty Twenty **54**

Ueland, Brenda **132**
Ulysses **85**
Unwin, Stanley **150, 152**

vanity publishing **151**
verbal slips **4**
visualization **7, 93–4**
voice **133–4**

Wambaugh, Joseph **5**
wordprocessors **2**
Wilson, Angus **109**
Wilson, Colin **45**
Wuthering Heights **25, 41, 90**
writer's block **142–45**
writing circles **141**

Zephaniah, Benjamin **97**

teach yourself®

Afrikaans
Access 2002
Accounting, Basic
Alexander Technique
Algebra
Arabic
Arabic Script, Beginner's
Aromatherapy
Astronomy
Bach Flower Remedies
Bengali
Better Chess
Better Handwriting
Biology
Body Language
Book Keeping
Book Keeping & Accounting
Brazilian Portuguese
Bridge
Buddhism
Buddhism, 101 Key Ideas
Bulgarian
Business Studies
Business Studies, 101 Key Ideas
C++
Calculus
Calligraphy
Cantonese
Card Games
Catalan
Chemistry, 101 Key Ideas
Chess
Chi Kung
Chinese
Chinese, Beginner's

Chinese Language, Life & Culture
Chinese Script, Beginner's
Christianity
Classical Music
Copywriting
Counselling
Creative Writing
Crime Fiction
Croatian
Crystal Healing
Czech
Danish
Desktop Publishing
Digital Photography
Digital Video & PC Editing
Drawing
Dream Interpretation
Dutch
Dutch, Beginner's
Dutch Dictionary
Dutch Grammar
Eastern Philosophy
ECDL
E-Commerce
Economics, 101 Key Ideas
Electronics
English, American (EFL)
English as a Foreign Language
English, Correct
English Grammar
English Grammar (EFL)
English, Instant, for French Speakers
English, Instant, for German Speakers
English, Instant, for Italian Speakers
English, Instant, for Spanish Speakers

English for International Business
English Language, Life & Culture
English Verbs
English Vocabulary
Ethics
Excel 2002
Feng Shui
Film Making
Film Studies
Finance for non-Financial Managers
Finnish
Flexible Working
Flower Arranging
French
French, Beginner's
French Grammar
French Grammar, Quick Fix
French, Instant
French, Improve your
French Language, Life & Culture
French Starter Kit
French Verbs
French Vocabulary
Gaelic
Gaelic Dictionary
Gardening
Genetics
Geology
German
German, Beginner's
German Grammar
German Grammar, Quick Fix
German, Instant
German, Improve your
German Language, Life & Culture
German Verbs
German Vocabulary
Go
Golf
Greek
Greek, Ancient
Greek, Beginner's
Greek, Instant
Greek, New Testament
Greek Script, Beginner's
Guitar
Gulf Arabic
Hand Reflexology
Hebrew, Biblical
Herbal Medicine
Hieroglyphics
Hindi
Hindi, Beginner's
Hindi Script, Beginner's

Hinduism
History, 101 Key Ideas
How to Win at Horse Racing
How to Win at Poker
HTML Publishing on the WWW
Human Anatomy & Physiology
Hungarian
Icelandic
Indian Head Massage
Indonesian
Information Technology, 101 Key Ideas
Internet, The
Irish
Islam
Italian
Italian, Beginner's
Italian Grammar
Italian Grammar, Quick Fix
Italian, Instant
Italian, Improve your
Italian Language, Life & Culture
Italian Verbs
Italian Vocabulary
Japanese
Japanese, Beginner's
Japanese, Instant
Japanese Language, Life & Culture
Japanese Script, Beginner's
Java
Jewellery Making
Judaism
Korean
Latin
Latin American Spanish
Latin, Beginner's
Latin Dictionary
Latin Grammar
Letter Writing Skills
Linguistics
Linguistics, 101 Key Ideas
Literature, 101 Key Ideas
Mahjong
Managing Stress
Marketing
Massage
Mathematics
Mathematics, Basic
Media Studies
Meditation
Mosaics
Music Theory
Needlecraft
Negotiating
Nepali

Norwegian
Origami
Panjabi
Persian, Modern
Philosophy
Philosophy of Mind
Philosophy of Religion
Philosophy of Science
Philosophy, 101 Key Ideas
Photography
Photoshop
Physics
Piano
Planets
Planning Your Wedding
Polish
Politics
Portuguese
Portuguese, Beginner's
Portuguese Grammar
Portuguese, Instant
Portuguese Language, Life & Culture
Postmodernism
Pottery
Powerpoint 2002
Presenting for Professionals
Project Management
Psychology
Psychology, 101 Key Ideas
Psychology, Applied
Quark Xpress
Quilting
Recruitment
Reflexology
Reiki
Relaxation
Retaining Staff
Romanian
Russian
Russian, Beginner's
Russian Grammar
Russian, Instant
Russian Language, Life & Culture
Russian Script, Beginner's
Sanskrit
Screenwriting
Serbian
Setting up a Small Business
Shorthand, Pitman 2000
Sikhism
Spanish
Spanish, Beginner's
Spanish Grammar
Spanish Grammar, Quick Fix

Spanish, Instant
Spanish, Improve your
Spanish Language, Life & Culture
Spanish Starter Kit
Spanish Verbs
Spanish Vocabulary
Speaking on Special Occasions
Speed Reading
Statistical Research
Statistics
Swahili
Swahili Dictionary
Swedish
Tagalog
Tai Chi
Tantric Sex
Teaching English as a Foreign Language
Teaching English One to One
Teams and Team-Working
Thai
Time Management
Tracing your Family History
Travel Writing
Trigonometry
Turkish
Turkish, Beginner's
Typing
Ukrainian
Urdu
Urdu Script, Beginner's
Vietnamese
Volcanoes
Watercolour Painting
Weight Control through Diet and
   Exercise
Welsh
Welsh Dictionary
Welsh Language, Life & Culture
Wills and Probate
Wine Tasting
Winning at Job Interviews
Word 2002
World Faiths
Writing a Novel
Writing for Children
Writing Poetry
Xhosa
Yoga
Zen
Zulu

teach
yourself

creative writing
dianne doubtfire

- Do you want to know more about the writing process?
- Are you eager to develop your talent and improve your skills?
- Do you want to find out about the industry and getting published?

Creative Writing is the ideal practical handbook for any aspiring author. Using exercises to explore topics, it will encourage you to develop, direct and edit your creative ideas in addition to giving you invaluable guidance on how to present work for publication.

The late **Dianne Doubtfire** was a successful author of both fiction and non-fiction. This edition has been fully revised and expanded by Ian Burton, a former pupil of Dianne's and a published author and lecturer in creative writing.

screenwriting
ray frensham

- Have you an idea for that script to end all scripts?
- Want to break into something but are not sure how it works?
- Do you need practical advice to improve your screenwriting skills?

Screenwriting shares with you Ray Frensham's extensive knowledge of this demanding but exciting industry. It takes you through the processes involved in transforming your ideas into a format that will really work on someone and shows you how to present your finished work to its best advantage.

Ray Frensham is a film and TV production finance broker and script adviser. He lectures and writes regularly on screenwriting.

better handwriting

rosemary sassoon & gunnlauger se briem

- Do you want to improve your handwriting techniques?
- Do you experience problems with writing and want help?
- Are you looking to experiment and develop your own style?

Better Handwriting is a practical and informative guide. The way we write mirrors our mood and character. It is the way we project ourselves to the world – and other people often judge us by our handwriting. This book is specifically written for adults and will help you to improve and develop a mature and individual style.

Rosemary Sassoon is a letterform consultant specializing in the educational and medical aspects of handwriting. She has a PhD from Reading University. Gunnlaugur SE Briam is an Icelandic designer and has a PhD from the Royal College of Art in London.

teach
yourself

letter writing skills
david james with anthony masters

- Do you want to write clear, persuasive letters?
- Do you want to communicate more confidently?
- Do you need to update your letter-writing style?

Letter Writing Skills is an invaluable guide to writing letters which say exactly what you want to say – and bring the desired response. It offers practical advice on layout, style and tone and examines different types of letter, from personal to business correspondence. A section on electronic communication helps you to make the most of email.

Anthony Masters is a writer of both adult and children's fiction and non-fiction books. He also runs writing workshops for adults and children.

travel writing
cynthia dial

- Do you want to travel the world... and get paid for it?
- Do you need help to find and present great story ideas?
- Do you want to turn your passion into a profession?

Travel Writing will give those who love to travel and long to write the essential tools to turn it into a career. Discover the steps you need to take to get started, the formula for writing winning travel articles, the markets available to you, how to get your work published and how to avoid common pitfalls.

Cynthia Dial has published hundreds of newspaper and magazine travel articles and teaches travel writing to a wide range of students.

teach yourself

writing for children
allan frewin jones & lesley pollinger

- Do you want to know more about the writing process?
- Are you eager to develop your talent and improve your skills?
- Do you want to find out about the industry and get published?

Writing for Children is the ideal practical handbook for any aspiring writer of children's books. Drawing on their own experiences, the authors offer you a professional's insight into the process of writing for children. Key points are demonstrated with a comprehensive range of examples and each chapter ends with suggested exercises to encourage you to apply what you have read and develop your own skills.

Allan Frewin Jones is a full-time writer of children's books and **Lesley Pollinger** is an author's agent and lecturer.